JEAN HERSEY

Cooking with Herbs

Charles Scribner's Sons   New York

*For Joan
whose fingers are very
green, indoors and out*

ACKNOWLEDGMENTS

Special appreciation goes to Gladys Ganzenmueller for her help in selecting recipes and in experimenting with some of them. Also for her generosity in sharing her knowledge and experience in growing herbs.

Particular thanks go to my husband, without whose advice and co-operation this book would not be.

I would also like to thank Martha White for her intelligent, meticulous typing of the manuscript.

Contents

Prologue

WHILE WE LIVE IN THE NOW, IN TODAY, OUR ROOTS DO stretch back and we constantly draw strength and wisdom from what has gone before, be it a few years, centuries, or eons. I'm thinking of herbs, and what they meant to people in the Middle Ages and before. Virgil grew sage for his bees, that their honey might have the distinctive flavor he enjoyed. Charlemagne loved to eat a blend of cheese and parsley seeds. Physicians through the years have healed all manner of ailments by skillfully mixing and using these plants. And of course there were the housewives who picturesquely brewed, poulticed, and cooked continually with herbs. We can picture, too, the secret concoctions of love charms and the strewing of herbs on the floors of castles and holy temples to air their healthful fragrances. Their powers, vast and broad, seemed unlimited. How vital they were to all people long, long ago.

I rather like the thought of this continuous flow from then to now and from now onward—the link with what was, leading on to what will be. In fascinating ways herbs met the needs of olden times and proved a delight and satisfaction to those who grew them. Many of the ancient ways and beliefs had enduring significance and are of use even now.

Building on the firm foundations of what has been, we find values for the current scene shining and relevant as today's sunlight, as the freshness of this particular morning.

Our excitement at the present moment is over the beauty and charm of indoor herb gardening and over the uses of herbs in foods. A special joy comes with the realization that we can grow many enchanting varieties indoors under our own roof. You can have this garden and eat it too! All winter long, all year actually.

So I lead you into a world perhaps unfamiliar to some, a world of newness, of nowness—a world of growing herbs indoors.

1
When, where, how

WHAT MAGIC LIES IN AN INDOOR HERB GARDEN! HALF-a-dozen or a dozen plants in the house create an oasis of green beauty and endless pleasure. Whether you grow them on a windowsill or on a table in front of a window, they present a scene of pure enchantment. Here the sun is back-lighting chartreuse leaves of basil and sending shadows from rosemary branches that form fascinating designs and patterns on your floor or kitchen counter. Next to this, ruffled, frilled parsley, green as the Irish countryside, mingles its tints with silvery-gray thyme. Beside the two stands a perky little chives plant with bright green spears thick as grass and pure white where they first emerge from the earth.

In the fall, when the outdoor gardens subside for the winter months, what we miss most of all are the scents of thriving plants and flowers, the aroma of the earth and the very fragrance of growth itself. But with herbs indoors your whole house is filled with delicious odors throughout the day all year round. Each time you walk past these plants, gently brush a leaf with your hand, and a pungent spiciness arises. A world of fragrance becomes yours overnight when you begin herb gardening. Touch a rose geranium leaf and your fingers hold the scent for minutes. After handling thyme a still different odor will follow you. How fresh and tangy are mint leaves—you need only draw near to catch a whiff. The smells of tarragon and marjoram vie with each other. Herbs are particularly aromatic after they have just been watered and the sun is shining on their foliage. What makes the plant release its pungent fragrance through the air or on the fingers is a mist of almost invisible drops of oil on every leaf.

Each herb plant also has a different texture from its neighbor. And the assorted varieties vary in shape as well as in tones of green.

Something about a herb garden in the house in winter fosters a particular intimacy between you and the plants. You are physically close to them and consequently more aware of each new leaf as it unfolds. It has been said that "Storms and winter weather bring plants and people close together." How true! I find myself with a warm affection for each of my herb plants and can't wait to take a look every morning to see what has gone on since yesterday. They grow fast. A little chives spear barely emerging from the soil one morning may be a half-inch up by the next.

Once you start a herb garden in the house, surprising and delightful things occur. For example, part of the past can be captured today in potpourris. The herbs you grow indoors provide some of the needed ingredients. Here in these aromatic jars, so at home in our grandmother's parlor years ago, are a delicious mingling of scents that refresh and relax. And you can now make your own tiny jars of captured fragrance.

Something else happens. All of a sudden your menus take a

new direction. Exotic but simple-to-make foods appear, to surprise and intrigue your family. Perhaps I should say that the ordinary foods you regularly serve suddenly take on an added dimension, something special in the way of flavor. Company meals have new character too. Of course, you can buy dried herbs in small jars for use in cooking. But like everything else edible, that which is home-grown tastes a lot better. Fresh herbs as seasoning impart a very particular taste that dried herbs lack (especially if they have been kept overly long). This is true of any garden produce compared with the same thing commercially grown.

We may regard lightly some of the lore about herbs. But modern nutritionists are now discovering the importance of these plants in our diets and in situations where they can actually meet some of our health needs. I suspect the physicians of long ago knew more than we sometimes give them credit for. We learn of sulphur in chives, and a high content of vitamins A and C in parsley. Some food experts say that the parsley itself may have more food value than what it garnishes. So never toss it casually aside on the plate.

Certain herbs are beneficial to nerves, others retard aging; different ones help bring health to various organs of the body. Each has some particular property of value to us as human beings. Many of the trace minerals and elements vital to us are found in these plants. When you cook with herbs, it is pleasantly reassuring to know that you are contributing to the general well-being of yourself and your family as well as adding a subtle and indefinable flavor to your meals.

Cooking is a thoroughly creative occupation! Half the delight of using herbs in food is experimenting. In addition to following the suggestions and recipes here, let loose your creative tendencies and try your own fresh ideas. Be guided by the general uses given with each herb. One vital point: herbs must be used sparingly. They are for the purpose of enhancing, not disguising, the native flavor of the carrots, the soup, or the roast. Incidentally, in cooking use twice as much fresh herbs as dried. An expert herbalist writes:

> *May lightning strike very soon*
> *The cook who measures herbs*
> *By tablespoon.*
> (FROM THE *Hemlock Hill Herbal,*
> PUBLISHED IN 1952.)

There's something especially inspiring about cooking with herbs. The flavors are so subtle. Their lore and background histories are so fascinating that you feel a little as if you're delving into magic—white magic. This is a kind of secret world, this world of flavoring with herbs—and a world where creativity runs riot. Cooking is always exciting, and the more romance and exotic touches you bring to it, the more interesting and stimulating it becomes!

We may live without poetry, music and art,
We may live without conscience and live without heart,
We may live without friends; we may live without books.
But civilized man cannot live without cooks.

OWEN MEREDITH

The first and most important aspect of raising herbs indoors is, where should they grow? The ideal spot is a window with full sun, but they will also do well in east or west windows. Certain sorts need semi-shade. Arrange these so they are sheltered from the bright rays by taller varieties that need to bask in streaming sunshine. Herbs can be planted in individual pots, either clay, plastic, or pottery (plastic or pottery hold the moisture longer). You can also get redwood planters in a number of different sizes and shapes and set the herbs in these. Arrange a half-dozen or so in one box, as you would in a small, outdoor garden. The planter may be a little too large for a window ledge, but it could be put somewhere on a table where it will get sun. For the most part herbs need to be cool, and when the weather outside is below freezing they thrive best with the foliage close to the glass but not actually touching it.

If you are an apartment dweller without much sunlight coming through your windows, you can still know the joys of growing herbs and of the flavors they impart to your meals. These plants will flourish equally as well under fluorescent lights as in sunlight. Get two 40-watt fluorescent tubes in a regular reflector. Set these about 20 inches above the surface of the pot soil. Keep the lights on fourteen to sixteen hours a day.

Certain fluorescent lights are designed particularly for plants. Among the best are those marked "Daylight," "Natural," "Cool White," or "Deluxe Warm White." The tubes will last about a year. They need to be wiped off every month to keep the best light coming through. In garden centers and through catalogs you will also discover there are special lights available to use over indoor plants that are sometimes called "growlights."

If by chance you should have a tiny greenhouse, herbs, of course, will flourish in it. They will also enhance any plant window, mingled with other indoor flowers. They do well in a bay window or on a sun porch. Somewhere, in everybody's home, is just the right place for an herb garden. And herbs are not at all difficult to grow.

A few general rules apply in keeping them flourishing and at their best. First, spray the foliage weekly, if not more often, with lukewarm water and a bulb sprayer. Keep the temperature in the area where they grow below seventy degrees if possible. Should insects invade and a spray be needed, use only Rotonone, as this is nontoxic.

A way to control insects that is far pleasanter and more fun than spraying is to buy a chameleon, or even a pair. Let them roam freely among the plants, which they will seldom leave. A little lizard will live there happily, licking water drops off the foliage with his pink tongue. He will also demolish mealy bugs, white flies, red spiders and just about every other insect house plants are subject to. In addition, this small creature will become quite a pet (and will never turn up in your bed, I promise!). He will sleep snug against a clay pot or under his favorite herb. He turns brown when relaxed, green when stirred up and excited—say, at the prospect of a mealy-bug dinner. I have never yet seen one turn plaid.

Herbs need ample room for root growth. Provide pots larger than seem necessary—larger than you would use for the average house plant. Almost every variety needs to be kept moist at all times, damp but never soggy. If I forget to water my chives plant one day, by the next the firm, upright spears of green are languidly trailing down. Happily, however, an hour after a half-cup of water they will stand up again! Although plastic and pottery containers do prevent the plants from drying out, I am rather partial to the looks and color of the terra-cotta clay ones. You will be equally successful with these if you remember that they need to be watered more often.

In raising herbs it's extremely important to keep their growth continuous. Hence an abundance of water is vital. You will be constantly trimming and cutting them for use in cooking and will want new, fresh foliage ever-emerging and the plant in a perpetual state of burgeoning.

[8]

Another fine point in keeping your herbs healthy is to provide them with fresh air daily. If the outdoor air is very cold, open a window in the next room, as they never like a direct draft. If possible, the humidity should be 30 to 50 percent. This is one reason why they do particularly well in a kitchen or bathroom. Frequent foliage spraying also meets their humidity needs. The ideal night temperature is fifty degrees, and never let the daytime heat rise above seventy-five.

The best soil for most herbs is average garden loam. Equal parts earth, sand, leaf mold, and well-rotted or pulverized manure. Never, never, never let the soil become bone-dry. Feed every three or four weeks unless directed differently in a particular separate chapter. A regular plant food may be purchased in a garden center.

Either arrange the pots in a tray of damp sand or pebbles, or set them in saucers of sand and pebbles. Never let water constantly touch the bottom of the container. The pot must always be above the wet level.

When should one have an herb garden? Any season is a good time. Winter, of course, is the season when window-gardening is the most exciting, but for those who live in cities what could be more appealing than a window-garden of herbs in summer too? They will do very well in front of a constantly open window. Growing herbs, then, is an all-year project.

If you live in the country or have a backyard garden, summer the herbs you have grown indoors outside in the earth. You can continue to use them in cooking. With annuals, it's best to begin over again each autumn. Plant fresh seed in the spring for the next winter's pot plants. The perennials, after a summer loose in the earth, may be lifted and divided, and new, smaller plants brought in the fall. It is a joy to raise your own herbs from seed, but if you are seeking a simpler, easier way or do not have an outdoor garden, you can buy plants each fall to start afresh. There are a number of herb centers throughout the country, places that skillfully pack and ship during almost any season. Magazines and newspapers advertise sources that will mail good-sized herb plants—a group especially selected for indoor growing. These often come in a complete kit, all potted and ready to grow. One outfit even supplies brackets for hanging them against the window and, as a final touch, scissors for snipping! Often, you can find certain varieties in the supermarket, in a nearby garden center, or at a farmers' market. Annually in the late fall, you're almost sure to see among the carrots and lettuces in your supermarket, rows of small, sturdy chives plants, each in its own pot. Friends with herb gardens are usually happy to divide some of their plants, as all gardeners find joy in sharing. If you buy herb plants you can create a garden overnight, and this is always a pleasure and surprise. What a welcome Christmas present these plants are, individually or in a complete kit of seeded pots or plants ready to harvest!

There is also another way of acquiring an herb garden that is rather intriguing and thoroughly satisfying. Raise them indoors from seed. How maternal you feel when small, almost invisible specks of green have just emerged from the earth in response to your care and tending—and, of course, to the spark of vitality lodged deeply in each single seed. Watch these tiny scraps of life develop into sturdy plants, and there you are, before too long, enjoying their lovely shapes and textures and trimming the foliage to enhance your menu. And you knew them first as seeds! Aristotle once said, "He who sees things grow from the beginning will have the best view of them."

There are a number of garden sources that make up kits for growing herbs from seed too. One day the postman may bring you a little unit composed of a half-dozen small pots, all settled together in a tray and the whole covered with a miniature plastic bubble. Each pot will be filled with earth just right for proper growth and nourishment. Little packets of different kinds of herb seed will be ready for you to sow. Sometimes the seeds have already been planted when you receive the kit. In either case, a little capsule of fertilizer is invariably part of the package.

With all these possibilities before you, growing herbs becomes irresistibly tempting. Don't even try to resist! Let not a day more pass before you commence this very special and distinctive adventure—an adventure in a new kind of window gardening and also in a new kind of cooking.

Happy Gardening

and

bon appétit!

2
Basil,
emblem of love and health

BASIL (OCIMUM BASILICUM)
MINT FAMILY (LABIATAE)

BASIL ORIGINATED IN THE TROPICS OF ASIA AND IN EUrope, where it still grows wild today. India is one of its native areas. This small, bushy plant has leaves of golden green, with a hint of chartreuse. Sometimes the foliage glistens with deeply scented drops of oil. The aroma suggests a combination of fresh, tree-ripened oranges, cloves, and licorice. The leaves are 1 to 2 inches long and pointed, and the plant grows to about a foot high in the house.

In days of old, people said that if you ate basil you would rapidly develop a cheerful and merry heart. According to an old-time custom if a woman in labor held in her hand a sprig of basil and the feather of a swallow, her baby would be born without pain! In Italy this herb was a love charm worn by the young peasants courting. If a girl gave her beau a sprig, she was certain to win his affections! And if he accepted her offering, he would love her forever.

Basil is a sacred herb in India, where it was planted near temples and homes to protect the inhabitants from evil and also to assure them guidance into heaven. A leaf placed on the breast of a Hindu at death was his special key to heaven. The mystics say of basil that when it is taken in food it quickly enters the bloodstream and there dispels all that is in opposition to life.

Today your small indoor basil plant will thrive and remain full and bushy if you never allow it to bloom or set seed! Fresh new leaves for use in seasoning will continue opening if you keep pinching out the tips of the branches. Leave at least two leaves where you cut, and new growth will appear in a week. Basil thrives in average garden loam rich in humus and well drained. Incorporate a handful of sand with soil in the pot. The plant does best in partial shade. Give a well-balanced plant food twice a month. Wash the leaves weekly with soap and water to keep free from insects. Be sure to rinse thoroughly, as you will be constantly using the foliage in your food.

Basil contributes zest and flavor to a variety of different foods. A few fresh leaves cut fine with scissors enhance salads and add a distinctive flavor to salad dressings. Add a few snips to canned soups or homemade ones. Use in stews and all meats and also in egg dishes. It is excellent in butter sauce with fish. Sprinkle it on fresh-cooked peas. It is delicious on boiled potatoes. A sprig of basil adds a pleasant tang to a glass of tomato juice. There is an old-time belief that a basil plant keeps the flies out of the room where it stands. Something to try!

Recipes Using Basil

ᴘᴘᴘ Mother's Salad Dressing

My favorite salad-dressing recipe is one I learned from my mother. I grew up with this, and I have used it with my own family ever since.

Pour into a jar ¾ cup of salad oil (I use safflower or sunflower seed oil. Olive oil can also be used.)
  Now add:

> A little less than 4 tablespoons apple-cider vinegar
>   (or lemon juice)
> Salt and pepper to taste
> 2 teaspoons brown sugar
> ⅛ teaspoon celery salt
> ⅛ teaspoon onion salt
> Dash of garlic salt
> ½ teaspoon finely cut basil leaves

Close the jar and give a good shake. Shake vigorously before each use.

If you keep this in the coldest part of the refrigerator, it will often thicken to a pleasant consistency for using.

Sometimes I mix in a teaspoon of mayonnaise before closing the jar. This dressing is not only our favorite on lettuce and mixed salads, but I use it in another way too. I spread it on both sides of baby beef liver before broiling. With the broiler door open, I watch the liver, turning it once, and take it out while the inside is still a little pink. It brings a superb taste to the meat.

Pork Chops en casserole

Serves four

Buy 4 pork chops, each 1 inch thick. Put in flat casserole. Salt and pepper to taste. Sprinkle 2 teaspoons fresh-chopped basil over the chops. Cover with foil. Bake in the oven at 350° F. for 1½ hours. Fifteen minutes before serving, remove foil. Five minutes before serving, spread ½ pint sour cream over the meat. Heat the sour cream, but do not boil.

Herb Tea Toast

Lightly butter a few slices of whole-wheat bread. Sprinkle with finely chopped basil. Put under broiler until light brown. Watch, as toast tends to burn.

This is delicious served with tea by the fire in midwinter, especially if it's peppermint tea sweetened with honey.

CREAM OF TURKEY SOUP

Serves four

>   3   tablespoons rice
>   1   cup water
>   3   stalks celery, cut up
>   2   chopped onions
>   6   mushrooms, chopped
>   Salt and pepper to taste
>   ½   teaspoon chopped basil
>   (Optional: a few snips of thyme and savory)
> 1 ½   cups cut-up leftover turkey
>   3   cups milk

Cook the rice in the water for 15 minutes. Add celery, onion, and mushrooms. Cook another 10 minutes, letting the celery remain a little crisp. Stir in the seasonings, the turkey, and the milk. You may also add leftover gravy and a little stuffing. Heat, but do not boil.

LIMA BEANS AND PEAS

Serves six to eight

>   1   large onion, chopped
>   1   small green pepper, chopped
>   4   tablespoons butter
>   1   pound lima beans, fresh or frozen
> 1 ½   pound peas, fresh or frozen
>   2   teaspoons cut-up basil
>   ½   cup water
>   5   tablespoons cream
>   Salt and pepper to taste

Sauté the chopped onion and green pepper in butter for 4 minutes in a deep skillet. Place the beans, peas, and basil on top of this. Pour in the water. Cover the pan and simmer until tender, adding more water if needed. Put in the cream, heat but do not boil, and season with salt and pepper.

ᴘᴘᴀ Sᴀʟᴍᴏɴ Sᴏᴜꜰꜰʟᴇ́

A special recipe and a favorite with the early settlers along the coast of the Carolinas   Serves four

Melt 3 tablespoons butter in a saucepan and stir in 2 tablespoons flour. Mix in 1 cup of cream and cook, stirring constantly, until thick and smooth. Season with salt and white pepper. Put in 1 teaspoon finely cut-up basil and ¼ teaspoon rosemary. Cool this sauce for a few minutes and beat in 3 well-beaten egg yolks. Fold in 1 cup cooked and flaked fresh (or canned) salmon. Last, fold in 4 stiffly beaten egg whites. Turn into a buttered soufflé dish and sprinkle with finely crumbled bacon. (If you like highly seasoned food, sprinkle also with ground black pepper.) Bake in moderate oven, 350° F., for 35 minutes. Serve immediately.

ᴘᴘᴀ Mᴜsʜʀᴏᴏᴍ-ᴀɴᴅ-Hᴀᴍ Oᴍᴇʟᴇᴛ

Special company breakfast or luncheon   Serves two or three

2 to 4	*eggs*
¼	*teaspoon fresh basil*
	Pepper to taste
1	*tablespoon milk or cream*
¼	*cup mushrooms, sliced*
½	*cup cooked, diced ham*

Beat eggs with basil and pepper. Stir in milk or cream. Cook in skillet. When eggs start to thicken, fold in sliced mushrooms and diced ham. Cook until eggs are firm. Parsley may be added.

3
Borage gives you courage

Borage (Borago officinalis)
Borage Family (Boraginaceae)

It has been said that "A garden without borage is like a heart without courage."

Borage is often called "bee bread" because it is so avidly sought after by bees. Another name for it is *starflower*. In

Wales it is called *Llanwenlys,* which means "herb of gladness." The plant grows wild throughout the Continent and England, where it flourishes in profusion along with cow parsley and ragged robin along the lanes in Devonshire.

Borage grows to 15 inches indoors. The blue-green leaves are covered with silvery-white hairs that shimmer in the sunlight. Stems are furry too, as are the buds. Leaves form in drooping clusters of lavender-pink, and as each bud lifts its head and opens its petals, it turns a heavenly blue. The flowers are star-shaped, with black cones of anthers. Occasionally here and there, some blossoms remain pink. Borage belongs to the same family as the forget-me-not, which also produces now-and-then a pink flower.

We grow borage in the window herb garden because of the beauty of the plant and its blossoms, as well as for its culinary uses. Few of our other herbs reach the bloom stage because we're always snipping off new tips for cooking.

Borage has several mysterious qualities. When grown among other plants, it is said to strengthen their resistance to disease and pests. What an asset! Also, it is known as the herb of courage. Old-time lore tells us that a tea brewed from the young leaves brings you, in addition to delectable flavor, great courage and verve. Before the Crusaders departed on their long journeys, they were customarily given a stirrup cup with borage leaves floating in it.

The French used borage to treat fevers and colds. A syrup made from the flowers was said to quiet the "lunatick" person. Raw leaves improved the blood and helped heal rheumatism, said the physicians of old. According to Pliny, a drink made from the leaves and blossoms made people glad and merry and drove away all sadness, dullness, and melancholy. The ancient Greeks and Romans put sprays of borage in their wine cups.

People today are discovering that this herb, when used in drinks, actually does have a wholesome and stimulating effect.

In the famous medieval tapestry known as "The Lady and the Unicorn," the borage flower, with its distinctive black center or "beauty spot," is depicted on the background. The blossoms of this herb also appear in some of the finest old English embroidery.

To grow borage in the house successfully, give it a moist, rich, well-drained soil and a sunny spot in the window. If seed is sown in the garden in spring, by fall a crop of small, sturdy young plants will self-sow near the parent. Pot these and bring them into the house; they will begin blooming by the new year and continue until spring. Discard them then because by that time they will have become too rangy. During the winter trim the stems back often to keep the plant shapely and prevent straggling. Borage is easy to raise from seed and will quite likely drop its own seed into neighboring pots, where young plants will soon sprout.

Small, new borage leaves are delicious in salads. Their flavor suggests mild cucumbers, and this cool, fresh taste makes them a favorite salad herb. In all dishes, use only young and tender foliage. The flowers, too, are edible, and delicious candied. Fresh-cut, they can be used to decorate green salad, potato salad, chicken or ham salad, and other dishes. Steeped in boiling water and then cooled, the leaves make a refreshing summer drink. Borage tea, hot or cold, stimulates the circulation and is soothing to the throat. The new tips of the stalks bring an enticing flavor to all soups.

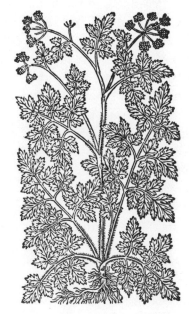

4

Chervil is for salads

CHERVIL (ANTHRISCUS CEREFOLIUM)
PARSLEY FAMILY (UMBELLIFERAE)

CHERVIL FLOURISHES WILD THROUGH MUCH OF SOUTHERN EUrope, and is said to be native to Asia. It has been grown for many centuries in English herb gardens, where it is reputed to have been introduced by the Romans. Often referred to as

[21]

"the gourmet parsley," it is a more delicate plant than parsley and has a more subtle flavor. In olden days it was said to be "exceedingly wholesome and charming to the spirits." Pliny recommended chervil as a fine herb to "comfort the cold stomach of the aged." It also is supposed to have great rejuvenating qualities. The roots of the herb were boiled and eaten as a safeguard against plague. In Europe light-green chervil soup is a customary favorite on Holy Thursday. With its reviving powers it symbolizes resurrection and new life and hence is appropriate for the rejoicing mood of Easter Sunday. Chervil was also called *Myrrhis* because the scent of its oil suggested the fragrance of myrrh, one of the offerings at the birth of Jesus.

Chervil grows to 15 inches indoors and has fernlike leaves with a slight waxiness. As the foliage matures, it turns dusty pink or lavender. The leaves are of a spreading nature. The flavor is somewhat suggestive of anise.

Chervil thrives in a moderately rich, light soil, but one that holds moisture. Give it sunlight filtered through neighboring, taller plants.

This herb has scores of uses. So often does it contribute its tangy zest to salads that it is frequently referred to as "salad chervil." The leaves chopped fine are especially ambrosial in potato salad. Chervil also enhances soups, especially sorrel or spinach soup. This herb may be used to add flavor to fish, eggs, meat, or vegetables. When the French say of any dish that it is *aux fines herbes,* chervil has had an important role in this mix. Europeans use it more freely than do the English or Americans. What a fine taste it conveys to puddings and butters, and also it lends a delicate note to vinegar and salad dressings. Besides enhancing all these foods, it is a decorative garnish for everything.

⌇SOUTHERN EGG CASSEROLE
Serves six

>   1   package frozen spinach or leftover beet or collard
>   greens
> 4 to 6 eggs
>   1   teaspoon cut-up chervil
>   Salt and pepper to taste

Place cooked greens in buttered casserole and make a depression for each egg. Break the eggs into the niches. Sprinkle with chervil, salt, and pepper. Bake in 325° F. oven until eggs are done.

⌇SUMMER SQUASH AND CHERVIL
Serves four

>   2   teaspoons butter
>   6   small summer squash (yellow crookneck or zucchini),
>   sliced
>   1   teaspoon fresh, cut-up chervil

Melt the butter in a frying pan, add sliced squash and chervil, cover tightly and cook over very low heat for 20 minutes. Watch carefully, as it may be necessary to add a little water at first, before the squash gives up its liquid.

CREAM OF SPINACH SOUP

Serves six heartily

¼   pound fresh spinach
     (or ½ package frozen)
1   teaspoon chopped chervil
1   chopped onion
3   cups chicken or beef broth
     (preferably homemade)
     Salt and pepper to taste
⅛   teaspoon nutmeg
1   tablespoon flour
1   tablespoon butter
1   cup cream

Cook spinach, chervil, onion, and broth together for 5 minutes. Strain and put the spinach and a cup of the liquid in a blender (if you don't have a blender, mash the spinach well). Return the blended spinach to the remaining broth and season with salt, pepper, and nutmeg. Add the flour and butter. At the last moment, add the cream and heat, but do not boil.

HAM LOAF

Serves six generously

¾   pound smoked ham
1 ½   pounds fresh pork
1   cup dry bread crumbs
     (crumble up your leftover loaf ends, using whole
       wheat if possible)
2   eggs
1   teaspoon chervil, chopped fine

Grind the ham and pork together. Stir all the ingredients together in a bowl. Shape into a loaf. Set in a baking pan.

Sauce for Basting
- ½ cup water
- ¾ cup light brown sugar
- ¾ cup apple-cider vinegar

Bake loaf in oven at 325° F. for 2 hours, basting frequently with sauce.

CREOLE MEAT LOAF

Serves six

- 1 medium-sized onion, chopped
- 1 tablespoon butter
- 1½ pounds ground meat
- 1 small jar red pimentoes, chopped
  (do not use the liquid; save for soups)
- 1 #2 can stewed tomatoes
- 1 teaspoon salt
- ¼ teaspoon pepper
- 1 teaspoon chervil
  (summer savory may be substituted for a change)
- ¼ cup bread crumbs
- 3 tablespoons flour

Sauté the onion lightly in butter. Mix all ingredients together in a bowl. If mixture seems too juicy to form into a loaf, add more flour and bread crumbs. Form into a loaf, wrap in wax paper, and fit into a bread pan. Bake 1 hour at 350° F. The wax paper will hold loaf together and help in removing it from the pan.

CHERVIL MARINADE FOR FISH

Serves four

½   cup vegetable oil (safflower, sunflower seed, or olive
      oil)
½   cup wine vinegar
1   small onion, minced
2   tablespoons cooking sherry
2   teaspoons chopped chervil
    Several sprigs chopped parsley
½   cup chopped, stuffed olives
1   teaspoon salt
¼   teaspoon pepper
1   pound fish (fillet of sole, haddock, or cod)

Mix all ingredients except fish. Add fish to marinade and leave for 4 hours. Bake in the marinade for 20 minutes at 375° F.

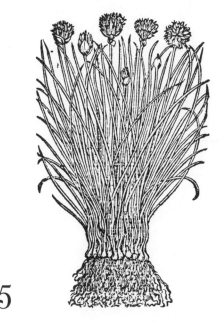

5

Chives for its gentle tang

Chives (Allium schoenoprasum)
Lily Family (Liliaceae)

Chives flourish wild in Corsica, Greece, England, Wales, and Italy. Records show that chives were in use two thousand years ago as a remedy for bleeding. This favorite herb was also planted in royal herb gardens throughout Europe during the Middle Ages. Nothing is more beautiful than the soft green drifts of flowering chives that carpet the southern mountain slopes in Italy. Here furry lavender flowers open by the thousands in the spring of the year.

Chives are rich in sulphur as are onions and thus provide our systems with this much needed element as well as with zestful flavor whenever we use it. People travel hundreds of miles, especially in Europe, to take curative baths in waters that abound in sulphur. Doctors tell us that this element is continually needed in the human system. Europe is a long way off! Now you can grow your own sulphur at home.

Surprisingly enough, with its onion scent the plant is a member of the lily family. A fountain of hollow, green cylindrical leaves emerges perpetually from its heart. Underground, each plant consists of a cluster of tiny "onions." Chives impart a delicate onion taste and smell to food. An extra bonus to its delightful flavor and fresh appearance are lavender pompom flowers. These somewhat suggest the clover blossom, and they appear off and on throughout the year. The green, upright stems are charming in the house in midwinter, when all too often the outdoor scene is gray and drab. This herb is so eager to grow that tiny new leaves of spring green are ever pushing up among the older stalks. It needs to be trimmed frequently for use.

Chives are among the easiest herbs to grow. If you buy the plant in the fall—and you will probably find it in your supermarket—transplant it immediately to a 4- or 5-inch pot of rich, moist, well-drained garden loam. It grows best in full sun and should never dry out.

Chives can be used just about anytime you would like a mild onion flavor in cooking. They add taste to soups, fish, eggs, meat, vegetables, and especially cheeses of all sorts. They're especially delectable on jellied or chilled soups, particularly vichyssoise. With a scissors, snip the foliage over the soup just before serving. Chives are also a great addition to salads and mashed potatoes. They do great things for a cheese soufflé and they add tang to potato salad. Dressings are improved with a touch of chives, and almost every dish looks prettier with a garnish of the bright-green spears, cut fine or left long.

Recipes Using Chives

ᖰᖰ᠊ HAMBURGER STROGANOFF

Serves five or six

- ¼ cup margarine
- 1 pound ground chuck
- ½ teaspoon celery salt
- 2 tablespoons flour
- 1 teaspoon salt
- ¼ teaspoon pepper
- ¼ teaspoon paprika
- 1 pound mushrooms, sliced
- 1 can cream of chicken soup, undiluted
- 1 cup sour cream
- 2 teaspoons chopped chives
  A few sprigs chopped parsley

Melt the margarine in a frying pan. Stir in the chuck, celery salt, flour, and seasonings. Add mushrooms and soup. Simmer uncovered for 10 minutes. Stir in the sour cream. Sprinkle with parsley and chives.

🌿 CHEESE SOUFFLÉ

Serves four

I have evolved this recipe by blending a few from different books and then adding touches of my own. It invariably rises satisfactorily. Sometimes its height and lightness are sensational. How high and light it will be, however, are entirely unpredictable! Minor variations in ingredients are responsible perhaps, but who knows?

4   *tablespoons butter*
2   *tablespoons whole-wheat flour*
1   *cup scalded milk*
    Dash of Worcestershire sauce
½   *teaspoon salt*
½   *teaspoon chopped chives*
    *(Optional: ½ teaspoon basil and a few sprigs of pars-
       ley, cut up)*
1   *cup grated cheese*
4   *egg yolks, beaten very light*
4   *egg whites, beaten stiff*

Melt the butter and add flour. Gradually stir in the scalded milk and continue stirring until thick and smooth. Add the Worcestershire, salt, chives, and other herbs (if they are being used) and then the cheese. Keep stirring until the mixture is smooth and then remove from the fire. Gently fold in the egg yolks. Let cool a little. Even more gently, fold in the whites. Spoon mixture into a buttered 7-inch soufflé dish. Set this in a pie plate of hot water. Bake in the oven 45 minutes at 325° F. Experiment a little with temperature in your oven, as it may take the soufflé a few minutes more or less to reach its height.

VEAL CHOPS AND CHIVES
Serves four

Take 4 veal chops (or pork chops), cut ½ inch thick. Lay them in a baking dish in about ¼ inch water. Add salt to taste. Put in a cold oven and immediately turn on to 350° F. Cook 1½ hours. Fifteen minutes before removing from the oven, spread about ½ teaspoon of chives over the surface of each chop. Add a layer of sour cream about ½ inch thick, completely covering each chop. (The little bit of water keeps the meat from drying out and seems to steam it into a state of delicious tenderness.)

BAKED ZUCCHINI

> 1 *small zucchini per person*
> 1 *slice ham per person*
> *Grated gruyère cheese*
> *Chives, cut up*
> *Butter*

Boil whole zucchinis in salted water for 15 to 20 minutes. When cooked, drain. Roll a slice of ham around each zucchini and place in a baking dish. Sprinkle with grated cheese and cut-up chives. Dot with butter. Bake at 450° F. for about 20 minutes, or until the cheese is golden.

JELLIED VEAL

Serves four to six

 2 pounds veal shank
 1 teaspoon salt
 ¼ teaspoon pepper
 1 bay leaf
 1 large onion, quartered
 3 stalks celery
 2 quarts water
 2 tablespoons gelatin
 2 tablespoons chopped chives
 (*2 tablespoons chopped parsley and ¼ teaspoon thyme
     may be added.*)

Cook veal, salt, pepper, bay leaf, onion, and celery in the water until the meat falls apart easily. Strain off the liquid and cut the meat into small pieces. Take one cup of the liquid and to it add the gelatin, which should be dissolved in ¼ cup water. Add the herbs to this liquid and pour over the meat. Put all this in a mold and chill in the refrigerator. When you serve, veal can be garnished with hard-boiled egg slices and wedges of tomato.

SPINACH PATTIES

This is an interesting way to cook spinach   Serves six

 1 cup chopped spinach
   (*or 1 package frozen*)
 1 teaspoon chopped chives
 1 egg

½   teaspoon salt
⅛   teaspoon pepper
1   teaspoon herb vinegar
½   cup bread crumbs

Wash and drain the spinach thoroughly. Stir all the ingredients except bread crumbs together in a bowl. Shape into 6 patties. Roll into fine bread crumbs. Sauté in butter in a covered skillet 5 minutes or so, until the spinach is cooked and patties are brown. Decorate with parsley.

AVOCADO DIP

2   avocados
½   teaspoon salt
¼   teaspoon pepper
1   tablespoon chopped parsley
1   teaspoon chopped chives
2   tablespoons mayonnaise
1 ½   teaspoons lemon juice
½   teaspoon paprika (for decoration)

Mash the avocados and mix with other ingredients except paprika, stirring well. Put in a bowl and sprinkle with paprika. Serve on a tray, surrounded by potato chips, cucumber sticks, cauliflower florettes, carrot slivers, and celery sticks.

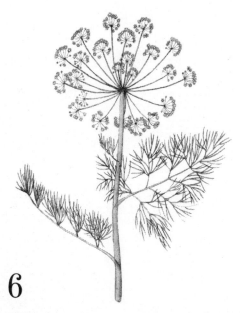

6
Dill keeps away witches

DILL (PEUCEDANUM GRAVEOLENS)
PARSLEY FAMILY (UMBELLIFERAE)

THE NAME DILL COMES FROM AN ANCIENT NORSE WORD, *dilla,* meaning "to lull." And this is an herb with soothing qualities. It is native to the Mediterranean shores and southern Russia. The golden flowers also grow in drifts through fields of corn in Spain, Portugal, and Italy. Dill is cultivated in Germany and Roumania, where the oil is used in perfume and soaps.

This sturdy, upright, branching annual grows indoors to 15 inches. The blue-green foliage is feathery, and the yellow flowers form in flat umbels reminiscent of Queen Anne's lace. The tiny petals fold inward, as if to protect some treasure within. Both seeds and leaves are of use in cookery, and the foliage, when handled, emits a pleasant and pungent fragrance. The whole plant is aromatic.

Magicians in days of old used to brew concoctions of dill for casting spells, and dill was also used as a charm to protect individuals from evil and witchcraft. As well as being soothing, the fragrance possesses a highly stimulating quality. It is said to stir and awaken the digestive glands, and the mere aroma creates a keen appetite! It is also reputed to shake the brain wide awake and to fire the will. Nor is that all. Like so many of the other herbs, dill also overcomes the oppressive and depressing feelings brought about by exhaustion or engendered by a close and stuffy atmosphere.

According to an old custom, burning dill drives away thunderclouds and clarifies misty air. In the human organism, it seems, there is a battle between the sulphur and iron processes in the blood. Dill, with its power of iron, helps to keep the blood's balance and acts as a mediator to keep peace in the human body—hence its reputation as an herb that soothes. A special brew of dill was used to send babies off to sleep practically in a moment—and restless adults too! Dill was the old-time sleeping medicine.

The early American settlers used to call dill seeds "meeting-house seeds" because they were carried to church and munched when the service was too long. What a happy answer to have something to put you gently to sleep instead of struggling to keep awake.

The poet Michael Drayton, in the seventeenth century, wrote:

> *There with her Vervain and her Dill*
> *That hindereth witchs of their will.*

The ancient Greeks and Romans burned dill as perfume and incense. The earliest record of dill being used medicinally goes back to 3000 B.C.! It is mentioned in an ancient Egyptian medical papyrus.

In olden days brides used to put a sprig of dill in their shoes with a dash of salt and wear a spray of the herb as well, all for good luck.

Give dill rich, well-drained, sandy soil and grow it in full sun. The herb self-sows. If it flowers indoors and you permit it to form seeds, it will drop these seeds in neighboring pots and soon you will have more plants. Seeds sown in the ground in the spring will provide plants to bring indoors in the fall.

Dill has a flavor like anise but more subtle.

> *A salad made with dill*
> *Is like a man of good will.*

Young leaves are cut up fine and sprinkled on salads, fish, meats, and soups. Dill is used the world over in pickling cucumbers. In Scandinavia a few sprays of the foliage are boiled with potatoes and peas. Chopped leaves add interesting flavor to butter or margarine. Dill is also delicious in sandwich spreads. Snip a few leaves into cottage cheese or cream cheese for an exotic and tangy flavor. Dill gives a subtle flavor to potato salad and tomato soup. Snip a few leaves over steaks and chops too. Try a little chopped dill in creamed chicken.

ᕈ SALMON FLUFF WITH DILL

Serves six generously

        4   eggs
        1   cup cracker crumbs
        2   cups milk
       ½   teaspoon salt
    1 ½   pounds fresh salmon
       ¼   cup parsley
            Several dill leaves, cut up fine
            A pinch of thyme

Beat eggs until light, stir in cracker crumbs, milk, and salt. Boil the salmon until tender, drain, and remove the bones and skin. Mix the salmon into the eggs. Add the parsley, dill, and thyme and spread into a buttered casserole. Bake in oven at 350° F. for 20 to 30 minutes, or until the mixture rises and browns. Serve at once with melted butter.

ᕈ DILL BUTTER SAUCE

To use on fish or meats

Cream ½ pound butter with 2 tablespoons dill leaves cut up fine. Add 2 tablespoons chopped parsley and ¼ teaspoon thyme. Mix well and store in refrigerator. Spread over a steak before you broil it; this imparts a delicious flavor.

7

Geraniums with their spicy aroma

SCENTED GERANIUM (PELARGONIUM)
GERANIUM FAMILY (GERANIACEAE)

P. graveolens. Frequently called rose geranium. It is the best known of the popular, fragrant varieties. The rich, green leaves are slightly frilled. When you touch a leaf, you release a delicious odor of roses and spice.

[38]

P. fragrans. Popularly called nutmeg geranium. Gray-green leaves with crinkled edges give off, when handled, a distinct odor of nutmeg.

P. tomentosum. Peppermint geranium. The rather large, flat leaves are covered with down that looks silver in the sunlight and when drops of water rest on it. Strongly aromatic.

P. capitatum. Attar of roses geranium. The foliage of this plant gives off one of the sweetest fragrances of any herb.

With their soft, velvety texture, the leaves of all geraniums suggest scraps of velvet, and each one is an invitation to touch. When you set off for your morning shopping, put a leaf in your purse (of any one of these varieties). Each time you open the bag a wonderful scent rises to greet and refresh you.

One of the places of origin for pelargoniums is the South African cape. Fields of scented geraniums also flourish in the south of France and are used for distillation into perfume. It takes a pound of leaves to produce a gram of oil.

Every herb has a special fragrance, but aromatic geraniums are an outstanding feature in an indoor garden as far as scent is concerned. You may be in the next room when an elusive fragrance wafts your way. Most likely it will be a member of this wonderful family.

About 300 years ago the first scented geraniums arrived in Europe, and about 100 years ago they were at the height of their popularity in America, where they turned nearly every sunny farmhouse kitchen window into a garden. In olden days people bathed an aching head with vinegar in which fragrant geranium leaves had been soaked. In the Victorian era, with its parlors and antimacassars and trailing potted ferns, one invariably found a potpourri in which scented geraniums played an important role. This would be a small, decorative jar with a cover, primly set somewhere on a gilt-leg table. Here, when you were a little girl, your grandmother or great-aunt would lift the top especially for you once in a while when you had been very, very good. She would let you take a long, lingering whiff.

These geraniums are having a popular revival today. They do best in full sun and at a temperature no higher than 72° F. Keep the plants neat and shapely by trimming off leaves for various uses. Grow them in rich garden loam. This is one of the few herbs that must dry out between thorough waterings. Grow geraniums in equal parts of garden loam, compost, leaf mold, and sand. Feed with a balanced plant food twice a month.

New plants of scented geraniums are readily made by cutting off a 4- to 6-inch stalk and settling it 2 inches deep in a pot of sandy soil. Place it in the window in the shade of other plants. When new leaves unfold, you will know that the new cutting has begun to root and it can be moved to sun.

Fragrant geraniums are used in teas, sachets, and potpourris. There are also several interesting recipes that call for geranium jelly. Rose geranium sugar is made by scattering the leaves in a pound of white sugar. Keep this in a closed jar. Ten or twelve leaves will give a good, strong scent, and the sugar may then be used for cooking. It is especially delectable in cookies, sponge cake, and herb tea. Any of the sweet-smelling geraniums made into tea is delightful on a winter afternoon. Rose geranium biscuits may be served at the same time and are delicious. They can be used for strawberry shortcake too.

Use cut-up rose geranium leaves in molded salads. Spread rose geranium jelly over baked ham during the last 15 minutes in the oven.

ᴘᴘᴘ Rose Geranium Tea Biscuits

1 ³⁄₄ cups cake flour
*   4 teaspoons tartrate or phosphate baking powder*
1 ¹⁄₄ teaspoons salt
*   2 tablespoons rose geranium sugar (see above)*
*   3 tablespoons butter*
* ³⁄₄ cup rich milk or cream*

Sift flour, salt, and baking powder together.

With your fingers, work the shortening into the dry ingredients until mixture is the consistency of corn meal. Pour the milk into this and stir carefully at first, and then vigorously, until all ingredients are well mixed. Total stirring time should be less than ½ minute. Knead quickly for another ½ minute. Pat the dough on a floured board gently, until it is about 1 inch thick. Cut with a biscuit cutter dipped in flour to prevent sticking. (Small juice cans with both ends cut out make excellent tea-size biscuit cutters.) Brush the tops with melted butter. Place on a greased baking sheet. Bake in a 425° F. oven about 12 minutes. To reheat, wrap in silver foil or in a closed paper bag sprinkled with water and place in oven at 425° F. for 10 or 15 minutes. These biscuits may be made ahead of time, covered with wax paper, and refrigerated until ready to bake. For added geranium flavor, cut up fine a few scented geranium leaves and mix with the dry ingredients.

ROSE GERANIUM JELLY

Place 3 leaves of rose geranium in a jelly jar and pour hot apple jelly over them.

There are several uses for this jelly. You use it in a jelly roll. You can also make an easy dessert by spreading a plain sponge cake or pound cake with the jelly as a frosting.

ROSE GERANIUM CHICKEN

Next time you have broiled chicken, spread rose geranium jelly over it during the last 15 minutes in the oven. This imparts a delicious and subtle flavor to the meat.

MOONSHINE GERANIUM CAKE

5   eggs, separated
¾   teaspoon cream of tartar
1   cup rose geranium sugar
1   pinch salt
1   cup cake flour
1   teaspoon vanilla

Beat whites of eggs to a foam, add cream of tartar, then beat until stiff. Add sugar gradually to whites, then add well-beaten egg yolks and salt. Gently fold in flour and flavoring. Bake in an angel-cake pan for 45 to 50 minutes at 300° F.

8

Lemon Verbena is for fragrance

Lemon Verbena (Lippia citriodoro)
Verbena Family (Verbenaceae)

LEMON VERBENA IS ONE OF THE FEW HERBS THAT ORIG-
inated on this side of the Atlantic. Native to Central and South
America, it thrives especially in Chile and Peru. The Spanish
conquistadors took it back to Spain, and it quickly spread
throughout Europe. In Latin America lemon verbena is called

herba luisa and is used for healing. In Guatemala the plant attains a height of 8 feet or more, and on the Isle of Wight, 15 feet! But don't be alarmed—if you start out with a small plant indoors in a pot, you can readily keep it to a manageable 18 inches, particularly if you occasionally prune and shape. And the trimmings have so many uses.

This favorite herb is a perennial with lanceolate, angular leaves 2 to 3 inches long. Grown indoors, they are yellow-green, outdoors, gray-green. Wherever they thrive they have very interesting veining. The whole plant emits a fresh, clean odor of lemons warmed in the sunshine. Lemon verbena is grown primarily for its fragrance.

Give it rich soil with plenty of well-rotted or dehydrated manure. Feed regularly every two weeks. Summer in the garden if convenient, and don't be alarmed if the leaves all drop off when it is returned to the house in the autumn. More will come—but before the first ones fall, pick them off for use in potpourris or teas. Wash the foliage weekly with lukewarm water. This plant is susceptible to white flies, which of course the chameleons will take care of if you have a pair. If one or two of these little lizards are not a part of your herb garden, spray the plant with Rotonone when necessary.

Lemon verbena adds a delicious lemon tang to stuffings, poultry, or fish. Cut up fine a few leaves and stir into cake or cookie batter before baking—and puddings too. The results are pure ambrosia. Make a wonderful herb butter by creaming ¼ or ½ pound of butter or margarine. Cut up fine several leaves, add to butter, and mix in well. Use this on toast or boiled potatoes. Spread over a steak before broiling. Lemon verbena also makes a wonderful herb tea. Cut up a few fresh leaves and steep, covered for ten minutes in boiling water. The herb is a great addition to potpourris. Wherever you like mint, try lemon verbena. It may be substituted in all the mint recipes.

9
Sweet Marjoram, scent from a goddess

SWEET MARJORAM (ORIGANUM MARJORANA)
MINT Family (LABIATAE)

THIS ERECT, BUSHY PLANT GROWS TO 1 FOOT. THE OVAL leaves are gray-green and velvety. Marjoram grows wild on the hillsides in Asia and in most of the countries bordering the Mediterranean. Its aroma fills the air for weeks and months on end. It also thrives in England.

This was a favorite herb of the ancient Greeks. They gave it a name meaning "joy of the mountains," an appropriate title because it flourished through the high-mountain meadows all over the country and on the Greek Islands. The Greeks planted sweet marjoram on the graves of their dead so that they would sleep in peace. They also crowned newly married couples with wreaths of marjoram, as it was believed to bring great peace wherever it was used. If it sprang up on a grave, it was a message to the family that the soul of the one beneath the soil was in a state of bliss in the next world.

Originally, sweet marjoram was called *amarkos* by the Greeks. There is a charming legend about a Greek youth called Amarkos who served the king of Cyprus. One day he accidentally broke a bottle of perfume. In terror he fainted and fell to the ground. The gods, looking kindly on the youth and to save him from being punished, transformed him into the herb that acquired his name.

According to another interesting legend this plant was raised by the goddess Venus on the shores of one of the Greek Islands. At the time Venus first planted it, it had no scent, but from the constant magic touch of the goddess it soon caught her fragrance.

Marjoram flourishes in light, medium-chalky soil. Give it sun part of the day only. This is the herb whose foliage needs a daily spray of warm water not only to keep it free of insect pests, but to provide the humidity needed for its health and vigorous growth. Keep the soil in the container evenly moist. Cuttings root easily. A 4- to 6-inch stalk set 2 inches deep soon becomes a new plant. While rooting, it should stand in the shade of taller, leafy herbs. One way to keep the dirt constantly moist is to cover the top soil with sphagnum moss and keep this damp.

Sweet marjoram has many uses in food. However, a little goes a long way, so snip sparingly. It contributes a fine flavor to soups, stuffings, eggs, potpourri, tea, meats, roast lamb, cheese dishes, hamburger, fish, stews, peas, and tomatoes. Add to boiled onions for a special treat and use lavishly as a garnish.

For herb toast, butter whole-wheat bread lightly, add a few cut-up leaves of sweet marjoram, and broil until toasted.

One way of cooking roast lamb is to combine 3 tablespoons of brown sugar with 1 teaspoon sweet marjoram. Sprinkle this evenly over the surface of lamb before it is baked, and insert a few whole cloves into the meat.

Recipes Using Marjoram

GREEN RICE SOUFFLÉ
Serves six

2   cups cooked brown rice
1   cup grated cheddar cheese
1   cup parsley, cut up
½   teaspoon marjoram
2   tablespoons chopped onions
    Salt and pepper to taste
3   eggs, separated

Mix rice, cheese, parsley, marjoram, onion, and salt and pepper. Beat egg yolks thoroughly until light and lemon-colored and fold into the rice and cheese mixture. Then gently blend in egg whites, beaten until stiff. Pour into a buttered soufflé dish, set in a pan of hot water. Bake at 350° F. for 25 minutes. Goes well with fish or veal or lamb.

ᵱᵱ Evergreen Salad

Serves twelve and makes a fine company supper served with hot whole-wheat rolls

10 cups mixed greens (Boston, iceberg, and romaine lettuce)
1 bunch watercress, cut up
2 slivered green peppers
5 stalks celery, chopped fine
1 bunch parsley, chopped
1 tablespoon chopped fresh marjoram
(*Optional: 1 tablespoon tarragon*)

Mix all ingredients in a huge salad bowl and toss with Mother's Salad Dressing (see page 14).

To make this a heartier salad, toss with cut-up ham, chicken, or turkey. Or add chopped bacon, chopped hard-boiled eggs, and cut-up tomatoes. Instead of chicken, turkey, or ham, cooked salmon makes an excellent addition to salad.

ᵱᵱ Meat Loaf

Serves six

This is my own blend of several recipes, plus a few additions that aren't in any of them.

1 ½ pounds ground beef
¼ pound veal
¼ pound pork
2 eggs
1 cup chopped parsley

¼	cup flour
2	tablespoons melted margarine or butter
2	tablespoons bread crumbs
2	teaspoons lemon juice
2	teaspoons salt
½	teaspoon onion powder or onion juice
½	teaspoon sweet marjoram

Stir and mix all ingredients well in a large bowl until you are sure everything is blended thoroughly. Shape into a loaf and wrap in wax paper. Fit into a bread pan. Bake for 1 hour in a 350° F. oven. The wax paper holds the juices in, and this meat loaf will be firm and hold its shape. It is just as good served hot or cold. Cold, it may be cut for sandwiches. It's also one of those convenient company dishes that you can prepare a day or two ahead and then cook just before dinner.

☙ Baked Eggs with Cheese

Makes a pleasant company breakfast. Each serving is mixed individually, so you can use 1 or 2 eggs, depending on your guests' appetites.

Into individual custard cup, or equivalent containers, break 1 or 2 eggs. Salt to taste. Add a few snips marjoram. Add 2 tablespoons cream and 2 tablespoons grated cheddar cheese. More (or less) cheese can be used. Bake at 350° F., testing frequently, until cheese is melted and eggs are cooked. This takes only a few minutes.

ℳ CORN PUDDING

Serves six

2	tablespoons margarine
1 ½	tablespoons flour
1	cup milk
1	#2 can cream-style corn
1	tablespoon brown sugar
1	teaspoon salt
¼	teaspoon marjoram
	(*Optional: 1 tablespoon parsley, chopped, and ¼ tea-spoon basil*)
2	eggs, well-beaten

Place the margarine in a skillet over low heat. Add flour and mix well. Pour in milk and stir into a smooth sauce. Put in corn, sugar, seasoning, and herbs. Heat and blend. Remove from the stove and fold in the well-beaten eggs. Pour into a buttered baking dish. Bake at 350° F. for 30 minutes, or until firm.

10
Mint is for refreshment

PEPPERMINT (MENTHACEAE)
MINT FAMILY (LABIATAE)

M. citrata—Lemon Mint
M. piperita—Regular Mint
M. rotundifolia—Apple Mint

MINT THRIVES NEAR WATER AND IS BELIEVED TO HAVE originated in the Mediterranean area—in the Greek Islands, along the shores of Spain, and in Italy and southern France. These herbs are members of an indomitable plant family. Unquenchable in their enthusiasm for growing, they are flamboyant and fascinating. Where you find them, they flourish in great sweeps, the roots woven together, thick as mats. The Crusaders brought many varieties back to Central Europe. The Pilgrim Fathers packed them in with the chickens and breadfruit and other treasures they took along when they sailed for America. The names and varieties of this plant family are legion and its uses practically uncountable. In addition, it is one of the easiest of all herbs to grow indoors.

What a refreshing and cool smell a single small mint plant imparts to the room in which it grows. As the new branch tips develop, they unfold pairs of leaves resembling small green roses. You can always recognize a mint plant, winter or summer, indoors or out, because of the square cross-section of the stems. Apple mint has pale green leaves that are soft and wooly and rounded, with the scent and flavor of russet apples. Lemon mint is said to enhance the perfume of any other plant in the vicinity where it grows. In the window garden it quickens and stimulates the aroma of all its neighbor herbs to even greater pungency.

Ancient lore tells us of Mytho, a beautiful nymph with whom Pluto, the god of the underworld, fell madly in love. Persephone, queen of the underworld, became extremely jealous and turned Mytho into the humble but fragrant mint. Subsequently, the plant flourished in the shadows, near running streams, and in moist areas, all of which suggest the underworld. Actually, mint also thrives in full sun. It joins the host of strewing herbs used in the olden days on the floors of churches, temples, and castles and in chambers where feasts and banquets were held. Imagine what a wonderful fragrance mint imparted to the worshippers and to the inhabitants of the castles, as it wafted through the air around them. The ancient Greeks and Romans used mint in baths and also ate it to comfort and strengthen the nerves. It was also especially valuable in perfuming the bodies of the athletes before the Olympic games, as the aroma was considered to be a source of strength. A participant smelling of mint would be in best form for winning.

Breathing in the essence of mint clears the head and quickens and arouses the senses. Mint flourished rampantly in the old monastery gardens in the Middle Ages. It was rubbed on one's teeth to whiten them, and it is still used in many of today's toothpastes. The ancients used it as a hair wash and also applied it with salt to a bite from a mad dog.

Irish physicians a hundred years ago used to say, "If you would be at all times merry, put a little mint in all your meat and drink." If you do, you would never, never be downhearted. But beware of eating over-much, they cautioned, lest you should die of excessive joy! The famous Kentucky mint julep no doubt derives from this background. Lacking that beverage, what can refresh one more quickly on a hot day than a sprig of mint in a tall glass of iced tea?

Apple and lemon mint, as well as the regular variety, have an affinity for lamb. A touch of mint adds greatly to fish sauces, fruit cups, cool drinks, candy, vegetables, pea soup, currant jelly, vinegars, French salad dressing, and, of course, best of all, teas. And never forget mint jelly.

🌿 MINT PUNCH

Makes about 4 quarts

1	cup whole mint leaves (*lemon, apple, or regular or a mixture*)
¾	cup brown sugar
2	cups water
4	tea bags of your favorite China tea
10	cups boiling water
2	six-ounce cans frozen orange juice
1	six-ounce can of peach or apricot nectar

Mix mint leaves, sugar, and 2 cups water in a large saucepan. Cook over low heat for 15 minutes. Put the tea bags into this hot mixture and add the boiling water. Cool. Remove the tea bags and add orange juice and peach or apricot nectar (and rum or white wine if you wish). Pour over a large piece of ice in a punch bowl.

🌿 MINTED CARROTS

Serves four generously

1	bunch carrots
¼	teaspoon sugar
	Salt and pepper to taste
⅛	cup sherry
1	tablespoon butter
1	teaspoon mint (*any variety or a mixture*)

Wash, scrape, and cut up the carrots. Cover with water and add sugar and salt and pepper. Cook until tender. Drain, add sherry and heat. Place in a serving dish with butter, stirring the carrots around in the butter. Sprinkle with mint and serve.

⤳MINTED SWEET POTATOES

Makes four large portions

- 6 medium sweet potatoes
- ¾ teaspoon salt
- 5 sprigs fresh mint
- ⅔ cup pineapple juice
- 4 tablespoons butter

Boil potatoes in salted water until tender. While they are cooking, cut mint leaves into fine pieces and steep in pineapple juice. Peel and mash the potatoes. Add butter and the pineapple-mint mixture. Beat all this together until light as a cloud.

⤳MINT JELLY

Take off stems and blossom ends from tart apples. Cut in quarters not quite covering with water. Cook until apples are soft. Drain and strain juice. Boil 20 minutes. For every cupful of juice, put in a cup of sugar during the boiling. While still cooking, put in a bunch of bruised mint leaves. Taste, and remove the mint when you have the flavor desired.

Proceed as with regular jelly.

Add green coloring.

☙ MINT CHOCOLATE JELLY

A delectable, cooling summer dessert   Serves four

1	envelope unflavored gelatin
¼	cup milk
1 ¾	cups milk
1	ounce chocolate
¾	cup brown sugar
1	teaspoon chopped mint leaves
⅛	teaspoon salt

Dissolve gelatin in ¼ cup milk. Scald the rest of the milk in a double boiler with the chocolate and sugar. When the chocolate has melted, stir in the gelatin. Beat with an eggbeater until smooth. Remove from the heat and add mint and salt. Pour into a mold or individual custard cups at once. Chill in the refrigerator. Serve with plain cream or whipped cream with a little vanilla in it.

11
Parsley for almost everything

PARSLEY IS NATIVE TO SARDINIA, TURKEY, ALGERIA, AND Lebanon. These areas are believed to be its original sources, and it still grows wild in those places today. The Romans probably brought parsley to England. In the castles and great houses during the Middle Ages they used to toss it into the moats and fishponds to heal the fish when they appeared to be ailing. Parsley is a favorite of hares and rabbits the world over.

The herb grows 6 to 10 inches in the house. The leaves, green as the Emerald Isle, are tightly curled. The Italian variety has leaves that are single and more fernlike. Both kinds are useful in dozens of ways. In the ancient days of Rome, parsley was used to crown victorious athletes. Today we crown our roasts with this delightful green!

Theocritus writes:

> *At Sparta's palace twenty beauteous mayds*
> *The pride of Greece, fresh garlands crowned their heads*
> *With hyacinths and twining parsley drest,*
> *Graced joyful Menelaus' marriage feast.*

In the early days, parsley was used widely in wreathmaking. At Greek banquets, chaplets of it were worn to absorb wine fumes and prevent men from becoming inebriated. It was also eaten after feasts to subdue the odors of garlic and onions. Chlorophyll for sweetening the breath is not a new idea!

A gloomy Greek legend relates the tale of the mythological hero Archemorus, who was carelessly left on the ground by his nurse and subsequently eaten by serpents. Parsley sprang up where his blood had spilled. Soon after there arose a superstition that "to be in need of parsley" meant you were hopelessly ill.

But there are cheerier tales of parsley from the ancient days. The Greeks also crowned their victors at the Isthmian Games with parsley wreaths. Greek warriors fed their chariot horses this herb to spur them to greater speed before a race. Somehow

I enjoy envisioning a great warrior, in all his shining armor, holding large bunches of parsley out to his horse!

All too often parsley decorating some culinary dish is set aside and left on the plate, uneaten. This should never be done because parsley abounds in nourishment. It is richer in vitamins A and C than are cod liver oil and oranges. It also has a great deal of iron and, eaten fresh, is helpful in treating anemia. Parsley tea is recommended to relieve rheumatism.

The seed sometimes takes three weeks to germinate. Why is it so slow? According to old-time lore because it goes seven times to the devil and back before it germinates, and he keeps some on the way because he likes it. And that's why it takes such a long time to sprout and emerge from the earth.

In Tudor times parsley was used to prevent baldness. To achieve the best results, a man had to sprinkle his head thoroughly with parsley seeds three nights of every year. This hardly seems often enough, but that was the custom!

Parsley thrives in partial shade or full sun. Give it the coolest part of the window garden. Grow in medium-rich earth, incorporating a little humus, and keep the soil evenly moist, always using warm water. Give it plenty of fresh air. Don't try to keep a pot of this herb longer than a year. Start with fresh seed or a new plant annually.

Parsley enhances salads, soups, casseroles, omelets, sauces, and all creamed vegetables. Use also in stews, eggs, and melted butter for potatoes. As a garnish, it makes any food more beautiful. Tea brewed from the foliage is delicious.

pp MARINATED STEAK ITALIAN STYLE

Serves four

Marinate 1½ pounds sirloin steak, cut ½ inch thick, in 1 cup olive or vegetable oil, with ½ cup parsley, minced, 1 chopped clove garlic, for 4 hours. Turn the steak from time to time. Sauté the meat in a skillet until browned to your liking. No additional oil or grease is needed in cooking.

pp FRESH GREEN PEA SOUP

Serves four or five

	Pea pods (a handful)
2	*medium onions, chopped*
1	*small head lettuce, shredded*
3	*sprigs parsley*
1	*tablespoon sugar*
1	*quart consommé*
	Salt and pepper
2	*cups green peas*
	Celery leaves
	(Optional: thyme and basil)
1	*tablespoon butter*
1	*tablespoon flour*
1	*cup cream*

Wash pea pods, cut in small pieces, and put in saucepan with onions, lettuce, parsley, and sugar. Cover with consommé, boil once, and then simmer until shells are soft. Add salt and pepper. Drain off liquor and save, discarding the pods. Cook peas and herbs together until tender. Put through a sieve and add to liquor. Blend melted butter and flour together, add to soup, and cook until slightly thickened. Then stir in heated cream.

⤳ BAKED STUFFED EGGS ON RICE

A lovely luncheon dish served with salad and homemade whole-wheat or corn muffins   Serves six

        6   hard-boiled eggs
        3   tablespoons mayonnaise
        1   teaspoon Worcestershire sauce
        ¼   teaspoon prepared mustard
             Salt and pepper to taste
        2   cups cooked rice
        ½   cup finely chopped parsley
        3   tablespoons butter
        3   tablespoons flour
        2   cups milk
        1   cup grated cheese
             (Optional: ½ teaspoon marjoram)

Use individual casseroles. Cut eggs in half. Mix egg yolks with mayonnaise and seasonings, as for deviled eggs. Mix rice and parsley and fill 6 individual, buttered casseroles. Put 2 egg halves in each casserole. Make white sauce with butter, flour, and milk. Blend in the cheese and marjoram and pour over rice and eggs. Bake at 350° F. for 10 to 15 minutes.

✐ BAKED SWORDFISH (OR HADDOCK)

Serves four

Place 1½ pounds swordfish in baking dish with ⅓ inch water. Scatter over it onion salt or chopped onions. Salt to taste. Spread a thin layer of butter over the fish surface. Cover with ⅓ cup chopped parsley. On top of this, spread 2 tablespoons of corn meal and bread crumbs. Bake in oven at 350° F. for about 20 minutes, or until browned and tender. This way swordfish will never become dry.

✐ HERB CONSOMMÉ WITH CROUTONS

Serves six

    2   large fresh mushrooms
    1   tablespoon parsley
          (Optional: 1 teaspoon chopped chives and ⅛ teaspoon
            thyme)
    1   tablespoon sherry
    4   cups beef stock (from beef bones cooked all day)
          Salt and pepper to taste

Cut the mushrooms into fine pieces and add with parsley (thyme and chives) and sherry to beef stock. Boil 15 minutes. Season to taste.

Garlic Croutons

    1   clove garlic, cut
    1   tablespoon butter
    2   slices whole-wheat bread, cut in ¼ inch cubes
          Grated cheese

Rub a cold frying pan with the cut clove of garlic. Add 1 tablespoon butter. Heat over fire until butter is hot. Drop in the cubed bread. Stir constantly until golden brown. Serve consommé with a sprinkle of grated cheese and croutons.

Dressing for Green Salads

½ pound bleu cheese
1 cup chopped green onions
½ cup chopped parsley
2 cups mayonnaise
1 cup sour cream
½ cup herb vinegar

Crumble cheese, mix with chopped onions and parsley, and blend with all other ingredients. Keep in a tightly covered jar in the refrigerator.

12

Rosemary for remembrance

ROSEMARY (ROSMARINUS OFFICINALIS)
MINT FAMILY (LABIATAE)

THERE ARE COUNTLESS REASONS FOR GROWING ROSEMARY: the legends, traditions, and charm of the plant, its fragrance, and, of course, its many uses. This herb is native to the rocky coast of Spain and Majorca, where it clothes the slopes like heather, reveling in the mild climate. The gray-green foliage blends with the ocean mist. In many spots it flourishes on the cliffs overhanging the water. *Rosemarinus* means "sea spray," or to put it even more poetically, "dew of the sea." Usually, a plant that grows by the salt water carries the scent of rosemary. This herb is also native to other parts of southern Europe, where the aroma and flavor are thoroughly enjoyed. Roman and Arabian physicians used rosemary for many ailments— practically everything from depression to gout. It flourished in the Hampton Court gardens in Tudor days.

Rosemary has a spicy, piny fragrance; both foliage and flowers are aromatic. In Europe it is used in eau de cologne. The plant grows to about 15 inches in the house, and the needlelike leaves suggest an evergreen. Some are gray, some are deep green. None have any stems. They can be shiny, narrow, or broad, and are silvery underneath. Soft blue flowers appear among the foliage in the spring.

Rosemary is an emblem of friendship and also stands for remembrance. A bride would carry rosemary from her family home to her new one with loving memories of where she grew up. A sprig laid in the bed-warming pan used to give the sheets a heavenly scent. It was also used as a strewing herb. Bees love it. The wood from the branches made excellent lutes. Comb your hair with a comb made from the wood of this herb, and it will keep you clear-headed, so runs the old belief.

Rosemary restores a lagging memory. It is also a good luck plant, and very versatile. Rosemary keeps off witches, protects you from the evil eye, and clears the air. It is used at weddings and funerals. It is said to guard a church, as well as the dead and living, from all harm. Hence it is burned as incense in many religious services.

Robert Herrick said of the rosemary branch:

> *Grow for two ends, it matters not at all,*
> *Be't for my bridal or my burial.*

Since it is the herb of fidelity, it is especially appropriate at weddings. The custom was to dip a stalk of rosemary in scented water and weave it into the bridal wreath. At the wedding feast, guests were given gilded branches, tied with ribbons of various colors, as symbols of love and loyalty.

No wedding cake was complete without a few chopped rosemary leaves added. I wonder how it tasted and what the cake was made of in those days. No matter what else it contained, the rosemary in it stimulated the brains of the bride and groom and all the guests who partook, strengthened their nerves, brought them wisdom, long life, and loyalty, and quickened their spirits and made them merry. As an added bonus, it promised to keep everyone young practically forever!

A lovely legend associates rosemary with the Virgin Mary. According to an old Spanish tale, the flowers were originally white, but turned blue when the Virgin threw her cloak over a bush of this herb. Hence its name: originally, Rose-Mary. It was also supposed to be a symbol of Christ's life on earth. It grew for thirty-three years, up to 6 feet in height, and then increased only in width.

One of my favorites of all the old-time uses of rosemary is the Greek students' custom of twining sprigs in their hair when studying for exams—to stimulate their brains and clear their heads.

People also said, "Put the leaves under thy bedde, and thou shalt be delivered of all evill dreames!"

Rosemary thrives in partial shade or full sun, in the coolest part of the window. Plant in light, evenly moist, well-drained, limy soil. Give it ample plant food regularly every two weeks. Cuttings root easily in sand or vermiculite. Take a 6-inch piece of healthy new wood and put it 2 inches deep in sandy soil or vermiculite. Give the plant a large pot. You do it a great favor if you sprinkle a little wood ashes from the fireplace over the soil occasionally. Give it chalk or lime every month or two, just a pinch on the earth surface, not touching stalk or leaves.

Rosemary has many uses in the kitchen. It deliciously flavors roast chicken, gravy with lamb, soups, stuffings, sauces, and salad dressings. It's a great addition to jellies and makes a delicious tea. Stick a fresh sprig of rosemary in a leg of lamb, veal, or poultry before roasting, or cut up the leaves and sprinkle over the meat before cooking. Also use on pork or roast beef. Chop up leaves and steep in white wine for a few days. Drink this to stimulate the brain and whole nervous system! For a special treat, chop rosemary leaves fine and mix in baking-powder biscuits before you bake them.

Recipes Using Rosemary

ᑭᕐᓐ ROSEMARY TOAST

Butter lightly a piece of whole-wheat bread (preferably homemade). Cut up rosemary leaves very fine and scatter over the bread. Broil until toasted, watching to keep from overbrowning.

☙ ROAST LAMB WITH ROSEMARY

> Lamb roast, leg or shoulder
> 2 tablespoons olive oil
> Salt and pepper to taste
> Flour
> ½ cup chicken broth
> ½ cup dry white wine
> 1 teaspoon garlic salt
> 2 teaspoons cut-up rosemary leaves

Rub the meat with oil, salt, pepper, and flour. Roast in oven at 350° F. for 1 hour. Mix broth, wine, garlic salt, and rosemary to form a sauce. Baste the meat often with this until it is cooked. Allow about 30 minutes to the pound from the time meat is first put in oven.

☙ CHERRY PIE

> Pastry for two-crust pie
> 3 ½ cups pitted red sour cherries
> 2 cups brown sugar
> 4 tablespoons flour
> 1 tablespoon lemon juice
> 6 one-inch sprigs rosemary

Prepare piecrust as for any fresh fruit pie. Mix cherries, sugar, flour, and lemon juice and spread over the bottom crust. Lay the rosemary on top of the cherries so the flavor will permeate during the cooking. Seal on top crust. Bake at 400° F. for 10 minutes, reduce temperature to 375°, and bake 40 minutes longer.

LIME JELLY WITH ROSEMARY

Delicious served with chicken or fish   Yield: about four jelly glasses

 1   cup boiling water
 1   tablespoon rosemary leaves, chopped fine
 3   cups brown sugar
 ⅓   cup lime juice
 ½   cup liquid pectin

Pour boiling water over the rosemary and steep for 15 minutes, covered. Combine in a large saucepan, sugar, lime juice, and the infusion of rosemary. Bring quickly to a boil and add pectin, stirring constantly. Boil hard ½ minute. Pour into small jelly glasses and cover with paraffin at once.

ROSEMARY CHICKEN GARNI

Serves six

 6   chicken breasts (3 whole or 6 halves)
     Salt and pepper to taste
     Butter, softened
 2   teaspoons finely chopped rosemary

Lay the breasts in a glass casserole that is fairly flat, with ½ inch water in the bottom. Season to taste, spread butter over meat, and sprinkle the rosemary on top. Cover with foil and cook for 1½ hours at 350° F., adding more water if necessary to keep moist. Take off foil and place under the broiler for the last 15 minutes of cooking.

13

Sage quickens the senses

SAGE (SALVIA OFFICINALIS)
MINT FAMILY (LABIATAE)

THE NAME SALVIA DERIVES FROM THE LATIN MEAN-
ing "healthy" or "well." In the Middle Ages the plant was referred to as *Salvia Salvatrix*, "Sage the savior." There's also a
pineapple sage for growing indoors called *Salvia rutilans*.

Sage originated in the Mediterranean region, where it still grows wild along the shore from Spain to the Adriatic and is especially prolific near Fiume. It also flourishes in Syria, throughout Italy, and in southern France.

The herb attains a height of 15 inches in the window. The leaves, gray-green, are a little nubbly to the touch, and the stems are stiff and woody. The whole plant is highly aromatic and has blue flowers that appear in whorls. Pineapple sage possesses a real pineapple flavor and scent and is a delight to grow and use in all the same ways as regular sage. An added bonus is its scarlet flowers in a window garden all fall.

The botanist John Gerard said that sage quickens the senses and memory and strengthens the sinews. This old-time herb of health was given to older people to keep them vigorous. At any age or during any period of life a little sage tea restores your vim. The herb is also said to turn gray hair back to black. Years ago physicians used it for just about everything from rheumatism, sore throats, and ulcers to tuberculosis! It is even said to alleviate grief. In England, near Southampton, stands a small churchyard where all the graves are planted with sage. How fragrant that must be to walk through. Sage honey was a luxury of ancient days. Sage tea is popular in China, where the people today often prefer it to their native brew.

A present-day Italian custom in rural areas is to eat this herb chopped up in bread and butter sandwiches. There was an ancient belief that a man could never die while the sage in his garden flourished. From this stems the couplet:

> *He that would live for aye*
> *Must eat sage in May.*

As a preserver of youth, sage is believed to not only restore memory and clear the mind, but also to improve eyesight.

"[Sage] made the lamp of life, so long as Nature lets it burn, burn brightly," said Sir John Hill. Rub your teeth with a sage leaf daily and never would they decay or ache, said a seventeenth-century physician.

In the window garden sage thrives in full sun or partial shade. Frequent fresh air is vital. Keep the soil constantly moist for an abundant crop of foliage. Grow in well-drained, average garden soil. Large plants may be divided in spring or fall, and reset in their pots in new earth. Both sages mentioned here do best in limy or sandy soil. Feed regularly every two or three weeks. In order to create a new plant, peg a stray branch down in a neighboring pot of dirt. Soon you'll have a young sage sprouting. As fresh leaves develop, cut from the parent.

A few sage leaves, cut up fine, are delicious not only in bread and butter sandwiches, but also in toasted cheese sandwiches—and a must in cheese soufflé. Sage is excellent for flavoring cheese dishes of all sorts. It is a great addition to stuffing, and it lends a delightful flavor to pork and poultry. The herb is a digestive and therefore of particular value with rich foods such as duck and goose. Fresh-picked sage added with onion to their stuffing is delectable. Or put a little sage in the turkey stuffing to help you digest and survive a rich Thanksgiving feast!

As an herb, sage is as important for its utilitarian uses as rosemary is for its aesthetic use.

Herb Bread

This is my own recipe, which I have evolved over the years through the process of trial and error.

      2 packages active dry yeast
      1 cup rolled oats
    2 ½ cups boiling water
         About 7 cups unbleached organic white flour (regular
             enriched white flour may be used)
      2 teaspoons salt
      2 tablespoons soft butter
      ½ cup molasses or honey
      2 teaspoons sage, cut up fine
      1 teaspoon marjoram, cut fine
      ½ teaspoon dried anise
      ⅓ cup lukewarm water

Let the yeast stand in warm water 5 minutes. Soak rolled oats in boiling water until lukewarm, about ½ hour. Mix in yeast and all other ingredients, including herbs. Knead and let rise, covered, in a warm place. Cut down after it has doubled in bulk. Divide into 2 well-buttered bread pans. Let rise again. Put in a cold oven and turn oven to 325° F. Bake about 1 hour, or until nicely brown. Butter the crust immediately upon removing from oven. Set on a wire rack to cool. Wrap in an airtight plastic bag. It will keep fresh a long time in the refrigerator. Makes heavenly toast and is particularly good in sandwiches or use for just plain bread and butter (especially with sweet butter).

☙ BEEF STEW

Serves six, with some left over. It is a whole meal in itself—and very special.

2	cloves garlic
⅓	cup oil
2	pounds lean beef (sirloin, round, or chuck)
½	pound lean lamb
½	pound lean veal
2	large onions, sliced
1	teaspoon chopped fresh sage leaves
1	tablespoon salt
¼	cup cut parsley
1	tablespoon butter
¾	cup dry red wine
1 ½	cups water, or enough to cover meat

Rub stew pot with cut cloves of garlic. Add oil and heat. Add meat, cut in 2-inch cubes, and onions. Brown well. Mix in herbs, butter, wine, and water. Cover and simmer 1½ hours, or until just tender.

1 ½	pounds shelled peas and a handful of pods
4	large tomatoes, quartered
8	small peeled onions
6	carrots, sliced
¾	pound mushrooms
1	cup water
	Salt and pepper to taste

Simmer the above ingredients 15 minutes. Add to stew pot and simmer everything together for 10 minutes.

ᴘᴘᴘ CHEESIES

> $\frac{1}{8}$ teaspoon salt
> $\frac{1}{4}$ pound sharp cheddar, grated
> $\frac{1}{8}$ cup margarine
> $\frac{1}{2}$ cup all-purpose flour
> 1   teaspoon fresh sage leaves, cut up

Mix all ingredients well. Form into a roll. Chill. Slice $\frac{1}{4}$ inch thick. Bake 8 minutes at 350° F. Allow to cool. Serve as an appetizer or with salad.

ᴘᴘᴘ SAGE SAUCE

For this you need 2 onions, 2 tablespoons butter, 1$\frac{1}{2}$ teaspoons flour, 1 cup of brown gravy, 1 teaspoon of vinegar, salt and pepper, 1 teaspoon chopped sage leaves. Melt the butter in a saucepan. Add flour, sage, and chopped onion. Cook for 10 minutes. Stir in the vinegar, salt and pepper, and gravy. Cook over low heat for $\frac{1}{2}$ hour. Use on roasts and reheated sliced meats of any kind and also on meat loaf.

14
Summer Savory, beloved by bees

Summer Savory (Satureia hortensis)
Mint Family (Labiatae)

Summer savory is native to the Mediterranean region. This herb, like many others, is well loved by bees. The Romans used it in sauces for fish and meat before other spices were available from the Orient.

The herb is charming indoors in the window. Narrow leaves appear on firm stems, turning the plant, as it develops, into a miniature tree. During the summer, tiny, pale-lavender and pink flowers appear like raindrops all through the foliage. The scent of the fresh-growing leaves suggests spices, camphor, and a touch of benzoin.

According to the ancients, summer savory belonged to the satyrs, wanton, woodland deities who wore wreaths of the plant as crowns. Poultices of savory and wheat flour were applied by physicians long ago to limbs aching with sciatica or rheumatism. If you heated a little savory with oil of roses and dripped it in the ears it was said to cure deafness. The early settlers in America brought this herb with them, along with other plants that they had relied upon at home. An application of brewed summer savory leaves was an old-time treatment used with success on fresh bee or wasp stings.

Summer savory thrives in full sun, in well-drained, average garden loam. It grows 6 to 10 inches indoors and is easy to raise. Give it a frequent foliage spray and, daily, a few minutes of fresh air from a window across the room.

This herb adds a wonderful flavor to green beans, in fact, all bean dishes. It improves the taste of soups, gravies, sauces for fish, and stuffings. It also makes a delicious tea. It adds spice to salads, meat, poultry, and sandwiches. Three tablespoons in $\frac{1}{2}$ pound of salted butter makes a savory butter for use on biscuits, scrambled eggs, or green beans. Summer savory also enhances egg dishes. Add $\frac{1}{4}$ teaspoon to five or six shirred eggs.

✒ ONION SOUP

Serves four

$\frac{1}{8}$ pound butter
2   cups sliced onions
    Salt and pepper to taste
1   teaspoon cut-up savory leaves
1   quart milk

Melt butter in a saucepan. Add onion, salt, pepper, and savory. Cover pan and cook until onions are tender, adding a little water if necessary. Add milk. Heat, but do not boil.

✒ LIMA BEANS WITH SUMMER SAVORY

Serves six

4   slices bacon
2   tablespoons bacon drippings
1 $\frac{1}{2}$ tablespoons flour
1   teaspoon salt
$\frac{1}{2}$ teaspoon chopped summer savory leaves
$\frac{1}{4}$ teaspoon pepper
2   cups water
3   cups shelled fresh lima beans (or frozen)
2   fresh tomatoes, sliced
2   tablespoons grated Parmesan cheese
     Chopped parsley

Fry bacon until crisp and dry. Put on paper towel to drain. Put 2 tablespoons drippings in casserole, stir in flour and seasonings until smooth, and pour in water gradually, stirring constantly until mixture is the consistency of thin white sauce. Add limas, cover, and bake at 350° F. until beans are tender. Cover top of casserole with sliced tomatoes. Sprinkle with cheese. Pile crumbled-up bacon in the center.

GREEN BEAN CASSEROLE
Serves six

Cook 2 packages of French-cut green beans until tender. Drain. Stir in 1 can mushroom soup (don't thin). Add 1 can Chinese water chestnuts. Stir in 2 tablespoons sherry and 1 teaspoon chopped summer savory.

Pour into casserole and sprinkle 1 can French-fried onions over top. Bake in 325° F. oven for 20 minutes.

STEWED TOMATOES
Serves six

To a #2 can stewed tomatoes add 1 cup raw celery, chopped fine, and ½ teaspoon chopped summer savory leaves. Cook until celery is tender, either simmering on top of stove or baking.

✎ BAKED CHICKEN LOAF

Serves eight

> One 4 to 5 pound stewing chicken (Cooked until meat
>   falls off the bones)
> 2 cups fine bread crumbs
> 1 cup cooked rice
> 1 cup chopped pimento (without the liquid)
> 4 eggs, beaten
> ½ teaspoon chopped summer savory leaves
>   Enough broth to moisten

Place the ingredients in a well-greased meat loaf baking dish. Cook
for 1½ hours at 350° F.

15
Tarragon
for its fresh sharp flavor

TARRAGON (ARTEMISIA DRACUNULUS)
ASTOR FAMILY (COMPOSITAE)

THE BOTANICAL NAME FOR TARRAGON COMES FROM THE
Latin word meaning "little dragon," because the coiled roots of
the plant suggest these creatures of myth and fairy tale. Because it was used for women's ailments, the rest of its name

comes from Artemis, or Diana, goddess of the hunt, of the moon, and of virginity. It grows wild from the Caucasus to eastern Asia. The herb was used widely in France long before being introduced into American cooking.

Pliny, who had a word for many herbs, said of this one that it prevented fatigue. All through the Middle Ages sprigs of the foliage were snugged down in the shoes before a pilgrim set forth on foot on a long journey. This promised that he would never tire. One variety of tarragon is said to have been worn by St. John the Baptist in the wilderness and to have protected him from all harm. Physicians long ago used tarragon, claiming it had the power to cure those bitten by poisonous snakes or stung by deadly insects. It was also a favorite herb of Charlemagne. It didn't reach England until Tudor days and at first was grown only in the royal gardens. The English doctors of the period said that when tarragon was used medicinally, it was a friend of the head, heart, and liver.

Tarragon smells like newly mown hay. It grows to 1 foot in the house, and the aroma also suggests anise. The plant, graceful and spreading, has smooth, 1 inch leaves.

Grow your pot of tarragon in full sun or partial shade. Give ordinary garden soil for the most pungent flavor, with a little gravel worked in. Too-rich soil dilutes the flavor. The plant must have good drainage. This is one of the few herbs that needs to dry out between waterings and remain dry for a day or two. Feed twice a month.

The young, tender tops are delicious in salads. Dried leaves contribute to potpourris. Fresh leaves add a fine flavor to poultry, soups, sauces, and vegetables. It is an essential ingredient in tartar sauce. Tarragon also enhances vinegar, omelets, steaks, and chops as well as stuffed egg dishes. The leaves are also used in a *fines herbes* mix.

✿ BUTTERY SHREDDED BEETS
Serves four

6	*medium beets*
½	*teaspoon salt*
¼	*teaspoon garlic salt*
⅛	*teaspoon pepper*
2	*tablespoons butter*
¼	*teaspoon tarragon*

Grate raw beets with medium grater. Place in skillet. Sprinkle with salt, garlic salt, and pepper. Dot with butter. Cover and simmer for 30 minutes until tender. Add tarragon during the last 10 minutes of cooking. Serve with lemon slices.

✿ GREEN MAYONNAISE

1 ¼	*cups mayonnaise*
2	*tablespoons chopped tarragon*
2	*tablespoons chopped parsley*
2	*tablespoons chopped chives*
2	*tablespoons chopped onions*
2	*tablespoons lemon juice*
3	*tablespoons sour cream*

Mix all this together thoroughly and store in the refrigerator.

Chicken Salad

Serves six

 4   cups cooked chicken, cut up
 ⅔   cup sliced celery hearts
 ¼   cup sour cream
 1   cup mayonnaise
 ⅓   cup minced green onions
 2   teaspoons tarragon leaves, cut up
     Chopped, cooked chicken livers

Mix all the ingredients together, using more or less mayonnaise according to your taste. You can make salad a day or two ahead. The flavor is enhanced when the ingredients have all blended with each other, after it has been in the refrigerator at least twenty-four hours.

Tarragon Fish Sauce

 3   teaspoons flour
 1   cup milk
     Salt and pepper to taste
 1   teaspoon capers
 2   teaspoons lemon juice
 ¾   teaspoon fresh cut-up tarragon leaves
 1   hard-boiled egg, chopped

Blend flour and milk until creamy. Add salt and pepper, capers, lemon juice, and tarragon. Simmer, stirring all the time until it thickens. Add chopped egg to sauce before serving. Excellent with white fish.

CARROTS WITH TARRAGON
Serves six

2 bunches small carrots
2 tablespoons butter
¼ teaspoon brown sugar
2 lettuce leaves
2 tablespoons chopped parsley
1 teaspoon chopped tarragon
2 tablespoons heavy cream
½ teaspoon salt
　　Pepper to taste

Wash carrots. Slice thin. Put in a frying pan, butter, sugar, and carrots. Cover with lettuce leaves, dripping with water. Cover pan and cook for 20 minutes (it may be necessary to add more water). Remove lettuce, add parsley, tarragon, cream, salt, and pepper.

CHICKEN WITH TARRAGON

Allow one chicken breast per serving. Brown in melted butter over medium heat, about ten minutes on each side. Transfer breasts to a shallow baking dish. Deglaze the skillet with dry white wine, pour over the chicken, and, if necessary, add more wine to come to about ¼ inch in the dish. Season with salt and pepper and sprinkle with chopped tarragon. Cover tightly and bake in a moderate oven for 30 minutes (be careful of steam when uncovering). Serve with plenty of boiled rice to sop up the gravy.

16 Thyme, symbol of energy and activity

THYME (THYMUS VULGARIS)
MINT FAMILY (LABIATAE)

THYME WAS ORIGINALLY FOUND THROUGHOUT THE TEMperate regions of the Azores, Corsica, England, France, Italy, and Russia. Many varieties of this herb grow along the mountain slopes of the Mediterranean, caught in niches between the

dry rocks that are open to the burning sun. It also thrives in the high mountain valleys of the Alps. The odor is so healing, it is said, that where wild thyme grows the air is pure as well as fragrant. In the mountain meadows you can "hear" a bank of thyme before you are close enough to see it. What you hear is the hum of hovering bees, who love it.

Thyme grows from 3 to 6 inches high. A particularly low and creeping variety is *Thymus Serpyllum*. This one snugs itself into the narrowest crevices of boulders. In a pot in the house, it trails and spills over the rim of the container.

Thymus vulgaris has dark-green leaves, each less than $\frac{1}{2}$ inch long, that occasionally have a gray cast, always glisten, and are deeply scented. The stems are white and woolly. Thyme and sage are two of the most useful herbs in cooking.

Thyme is an herb that has been associated with bees perhaps from the days of ancient Greece, when the most sought-after honey came from Mount Hymettus, a mountain carpeted with this wild herb. It also flourished on Mount Hybla in Sicily, and honey from both places was much in demand. Alfred Noyes speaks of

> . . . *the little blue wreath of incense*
> *That the wild thyme breathes to the sky.*

In Europe, years back, thyme symbolized courage, energy, and activity. In medieval days when a lady embroidered a scarf for her knight to wear in battle, the design on it was often a bee hovering over a sprig of thyme. Thyme, worn by young girls in those days, was sure to bring them sweethearts.

According to tradition, thyme was part of the straw bed of the Virgin Mary and the Christ Child. It was a manger herb and is always included in Nativity scenes. When Christmas comes, include a spray of the tiny leaves in your own small crèche.

Thyme is said to cure melancholy. It had many medicinal uses in the olden days, such as strengthening the lungs, healing coughs, and benefitting sciatica, dullness of sight, and gout. It is said to be soothing to nervous disorders. Drink a cup of thyme tea and it's a promise you will have no nightmares! It also wards off colds. All through Europe it abounds in orchard grass, drawing the bees and assuring good pollination of the fruit. But more than this, the combined scent of apple blossoms and thyme is enough to inspire the most practical of us to poetry.

There's a recipe from the seventeenth century for a way of using thyme in your food to enable you to see fairies and elves if you should be so inclined. This thyme recipe may be found in a museum at Oxford in England today.

Thyme thrives in sun and semishade. Plant it in chalky, sandy soil that is well drained. It is said that the delicate flavor of mutton from areas where thyme grows thick is due to the large amount of this herb consumed by the sheep. Thyme is adaptable and will do well in almost any soil. You can divide the plant at the roots. If it is permitted to go to seed, you will find new young plants springing up in neighboring pots.

Use this herb as freely as salt—in other words, in practically everything. Both varieties mentioned here make excellent tea. Steep a teaspoon of fresh thyme leaves in a cup of boiling water as a remedy for a headache. It makes a wonderful sauce for meat and fish and is used in croquettes, chipped beef, fricasseed chicken, pork, and soup. Thyme also adds a delicious flavor to cheese dishes, carrots, peas, and creamed onions. Sometime when you're feeling in an exotic mood, toss a few leaves into your hot bath, and be sure to add a little of the foliage to the next kind of jelly you make. One-half teaspoon of thyme leaves, cut up and blended with ¼ pound of butter is delicious when spread over a steak before you broil it.

An old Greek satirist wrote, "A cook is fully as successful and important as a poet."

Recipes Using Thyme

⚘ Bean and Beef Casserole

Serves eight

½ cup minced onions
½ cup diced celery
¼ cup chopped green pepper
1 pound ground beef
2 tablespoons butter
1 8-ounce can tomato soup
½ cup water
1 clove garlic, crushed
2 tablespoons basil vinegar
1 teaspoon dry mustard
½ teaspoon thyme
2 tablespoons brown sugar
Salt and pepper to taste
1 #2 can pork and beans in molasses

Sauté onions, celery, pepper, and meat in 2 tablespoons butter. Add soup, water, and the remaining ingredients except for the beans. Mix well. Stir in beans and bake for 45 minutes at 375° F.

JELLIED HAM LOAF

Serves six

   1   *tablespoon gelatin*
   ¼   *cup cold water*
   2   *cups ground ham*
   ½   *green pepper, chopped*
   1   *medium onion, chopped*
   2   *hard-boiled eggs, chopped*
   2   *sprigs parsley*
   3   *sprigs thyme*
   1   *cup mayonnaise*
   1   *teaspoon lemon juice*
      Salt and pepper to taste

Soften gelatin in cold water and dissolve in top of double boiler. Add the rest of the ingredients, mixing thoroughly, and pour into a mold that you have dipped in cold water. Takes half-a-day or longer to jell. Make a sauce of ½ pint sour cream, 2 tablespoons well-drained chopped cucumber, ½ teaspoon salt, and 2 teaspoons brown sugar. Pour over the top of the molded ham and then sprinkle with finely chopped chives.

BLUEBERRY PIE

      Pastry for 2-crust pie
   4   *cups blueberries*
 1 ½   *cups brown sugar*
   4   *tablespoons flour*
   2   *tablespoons lemon juice*
   1   *teaspoon thyme, soaked in lemon juice*

Prepare crust as you would for any fresh fruit pie. Mix ingredients together, saving the lemon juice and thyme to sprinkle on the surface of the fruit before you put the top crust on. Sour cream may be served with the pie. (Another fruit can also be substituted for blueberries.)

PORK CHOPS WITH THYME

Serves six

¼	cup flour
1	teaspoon salt
6	loin pork chops
1	tablespoon salad oil
1	cup fresh-squeezed orange juice
1	tablespoon grated orange rind
1	tablespoon brown sugar
1	teaspoon flour
½	teaspoon thyme

Mix flour and salt. Cover chops with flour mixture and brown in hot salad oil. Pour off all fat. Add ½ cup orange juice to chops and simmer 45 minutes, adding water if necessary. Remove meat from pan and keep hot in oven. Mix remaining ½ cup orange juice, rind, sugar, flour, and thyme together until smooth. Cook in skillet in which chops were cooked. Pour over chops and serve.

🌿 Sour Cream Chicken Salad

Serves six

  1   tablespoon gelatin
  ¼   cup cold water
  1   cup clear chicken broth
  1 ½   cups diced, cooked chicken breasts
  ⅓   cup chopped celery
  1 ½   cups green seedless grapes
  ½   pint sour cream
  ⅓   cup mayonnaise
  1   tablespoon each chopped chives and parsley
  ½   teaspoon thyme
      Salt and pepper to taste

Soften gelatin in cold water and dissolve in hot chicken broth. Cool, then stir in balance of ingredients, mixing well. Put in a mold. Chill. Garnish with watercress.

🌿 Spring Salad Dressing

  ⅓   cup chopped green onions (*tops and all*)
  1   cup mayonnaise
  1   grated clove garlic
  1   cup chopped parsley
  ½   cup sour cream
  ½   teaspoon Worcestershire sauce
  ½   teaspoon basil
  ¼   teaspoon thyme
  1   tablespoon lemon juice

Combine ingredients and serve with tomato-aspic salad filled with shrimp or vegetables. Or use on other salads.

17
HerbTeas

THE VARIED AROMAS OF HERB TEAS SUGGEST TO ME THE FRA-
grance of a meadow in summer. In the sunlight among the
daisies and black-eyed susans, there is one kind of scent.
Across by the stone wall, where the maples stand, the little
chipmunks run in and out of the rocks, and the sweet fern
thrives, another fragrance wafts through the air. What a clean,

cool scent comes from the freshly running brook and the area near it. When the field is newly mowed and the warm hay lies row on row, creating patterns over its rolling contours, an altogether fresh new pungency rises from the earth. And in the rain, something else again greets our senses.

Yet overall, and throughout the meadow, rain or shine, there weaves a kind of symphony of fragrances, perhaps the essence of the outdoors—of all growth, of all harvests.

This is the way I feel about herb teas. They are meadow grass and cool mosses, sunshine and rain, growing and harvest, and something of the very earth itself. Each one is a little different from the next. From every kind of herb tea emerges a special and unique smell and taste. Blended, they have a whole concert of flavors, all subtle, all to be savored.

Like many other treasures in life, herb teas do not flaunt their virtues at you. You must sip them in some quiet mood, during a reflective period in your day, when you are in a serene and receiving state of mind. Then, and then only, can you appreciate their subtle aroma, their delicate flavor.

On a winter afternoon by the fire, peppermint tea sweetened with honey (always sweeten herb teas with honey) and thin slices of homemade herb bread induce a beautiful state of peace and relaxation. In summer, on the terrace, what could be more appealing than iced geranium leaf tea with a few drops of lemon juice and a sprig of lemon verbena?

I remember a small inn in Switzerland high in the Alps. Here we frequently sat on the terrace after supper and sipped mint tea from fresh-gathered leaves that grew along the fence behind the hotel, where the wild lupin spread. That Alpine mint had a particular flavor all its own—from those light green leaves steeped there in boiling water. We and our friends talked and tasted. And all the while the sun slid down in the distance, behind the Bernese Oberlands, sending on the opposite side of the heavens an Alpine glow over the Matterhorn and the Dents Blancs.

There was the linden blossom tea we drank for breakfast in Holland too, and camomile tea in France. Europeans are far more aware of and appreciative of herb teas than are Americans, though recently we have become more and more aware of all the uses of herbs.

> *The Muses' friend, tea, does our fancy aid,*
> *Repress those vapours which the head invade*
> *And keep that palace of the soul serene.*
>
> EDMUND WALLER

The winter tea hour where I live, in North Carolina, is the time of day when the mountains stand sharply silhouetted against the orange sky. Here I sit with friends by the fire and look out at the line of ridges. Half the delight of herb tea is the aroma that rises while you sip. We may be having herb toast too. Or perhaps I have made herb cookies sweetened with homemade rose geranium jelly. There's a congeniality about drinking herb tea on a cold afternoon, a relaxation and a drawing together in spirit of a few close friends.

Mint teas are perhaps the best known of the herb teas and the ones with the strongest, tangiest flavor. *Mentha piperita* creates the most pungent taste. Apple mint is equally delicious, and lemon mint also. A blend of the three is intriguing. There is a definite restorative quality in mint teas. How refreshing they can be after a tiring day. Nothing disperses a headache more rapidly. If your stomach feels upset, a cup of peppermint tea will help firm it down again.

Rose geranium tea is another favorite of mine. This is a tea that is not only refreshing, but actually proves stimulating.

Add a dash of nutmeg or a few cloves to the pot for an exotic note.

Lemon verbena tea is especially appealing. If you feel a cold coming on, it can be most beneficial to settle in bed for a day or so, or at least relax quietly in the house, and enjoy this delicious tea at intervals. Probably, the cold will never fully arrive.

Rosemary tea is a particular must—for flavor, for the scent that rises from the cup, and also for some of its reputed powers. Again it was Pliny who recommended it for poor vision and a slipping memory. So while you're enjoying the piney, meadowy fragrance and flavor of this particular variety, made from a plant in your window garden, you can also be adding to your physical well-being.

Sage tea, another of my choices, is always pleasant to sip. Remember the adage that sage keeps you young and vital all your days on earth!

A few leaves of lemon verbena added to sage tea when it is steeping lends a fine scent and flavor. This is said to be particularly soothing to the nerves. After a rushed day, pause for a cup of sage-and-lemon verbena tea to restore your peace of mind.

Half the fun of herb teas is creating your own, trying a few leaves of this and a few of that from your indoor herb garden. A few marjoram and basil leaves added to most of the teas bring an unusual tang to the flavor. Parsley tea is delicious, and is said to be especially beneficial for arthritis. This is a tea you bring to a boil and let simmer for ten or fifteen minutes and then sweeten with honey.

Iced borage tea is a fine, cooling drink on a hot summer afternoon.

The way to make herb teas is to take the fresh leaves, cut them up fine with a scissors, and pour boiling water over them.

Let stand in a china or earthenware pot (not a metal saucepan), covered, for ten or fifteen minutes. If you set the pot on an electric burner that has been turned off and has partly cooled, or over a pilot light, the teas will retain their heat as they steep. You can also use whole leaves, as they do at my favorite inn in the Alps.

If you are firmly wedded to the regular China teas, for variety try adding a few herbs to these. All the herbs mentioned here bring a special note of interest to the Oriental varieties. Once you get started with herb teas, you may, like me, prefer them altogether to the conventional sort.

18
Miniature Potpourris

As TINY VASES CREATE ENCHANTING DIMINUTIVE BOUQUETS, so too do small potpourris bring you a touch of special garden magic. Lift the cover and take a whiff and your hour is made, so refreshing is the scent!

A potpourri made from an indoor herb garden must, of necessity, be small, because you can't use up too much of each plant all at once. First, seek out some miniature, decorative jars with covers. Japanese shops are a prolific source if there are any in your vicinity.

You can have as much fun being original and creative as you fill these little fragrant jars as you have had in cooking with herbs. Experiment with all sorts of different mixes, using your intuition and imagination.

In the days of old, people blended bags of sweet, spiced mixtures to wear, to carry, to put in clothes presses, and to keep about in their castles and manor houses. Their general purpose was to freshen the air in a room. In addition to strewing sweet herbs over the hard cold stone or earthen floors to enhance the scent and general atmosphere, people of old created jars and containers of herbs with wonderful aromas! In these covered china jars were the exotic scents of flowers, foliage, woods, and the earth itself. Here was the pungency of growing things, along with spices from the romantic Orient. Often these bottled essences suggested the odor of incense from some vast cathedral nave. And all these fragrances can waken and quicken the imagination and stir the wanderlust. Standing in your own living room you may find your spirits loosed and set to roam over mountains and seas and back through generations to the age of myrrh and incense.

A potpourri in your house, standing on a table, invites you to lift the top off every so often and take a deep breath. How pleasant this is. Sometimes a headache will steal away, unnoticed, as you inhale. Or maybe a sudden relaxation will spread through your limbs if you take the time for a few deep breaths of the fragrant and spicy contents.

Just to start off, here are a few recipes for using the herbs in this book in potpourris. In addition to the foliage, you will need a few spices from the kitchen shelf and also some dried rose petals, which can be purchased in any season at herb gardens and herb centers. Of course, if you grow roses you can dry your own petals in the summer, putting them on a wire screen, out of the wind, for several days.

The foliage from the herbs in your indoor garden must also be dried before you begin. Spread the leaves you have chosen on a wire cake rack in a warm corner of the house until dry and crisp. It may take a week or two, or just a few days, depending on the humidity in the air. There must be no particle of moisture, however, when you start. If a mold starts, all is lost.

Recipes for Potpourris

GERANIUM POTPOURRI

   3   *tablespoons dried rose geranium leaves*
      A few leaves of all the other varieties: nutmeg, apple,
        mint, and any other scented geraniums
      A few dried January jasmine flowers
   1   *tablespoon orris root*
   3   *drops geranium oil*
   1   *cup rose petals*

Stir all these ingredients together and mix in cup of rose petals. If you are using a glass jar, for extra color add a few dried blossoms of bright red geraniums, deep-blue delphinium, or bachelor buttons, and also a few dried sweet violets. Dried lemon and orange blossoms are also a great addition to a geranium potpourri.

✒ VERBENA POTPOURRI

2   tablespoons dried, crumbled verbena leaves
1   tablespoon thyme
1   teaspoon orris root
2   drops lemon verbena oil

If you are using a small, covered glass jar, for an interesting color effect add 1 teaspoon each of dried marigold or chrysanthemum petals, January jasmine, gardenia, lavender blossom, and sweet olive. If it's too late for your own garden to produce these, a flower or two from the florist will add the note of enchanting color. To this mixture add 1 teaspoon of dried mint leaves, $\frac{1}{8}$ teaspoon cinnamon, and an equal amount of allspice.

✒ BASIL AND SWEET MARJORAM POTPOURRI

$\frac{1}{2}$ cup dried rose petals
    A few dried carnation flowers (the white are the most
        fragrant)
1   teaspoon (or a few leaves) each of thyme, rosemary,
        sweet marjoram, basil, scented geraniums, and
        lemon verbena
2   crushed bay leaves
$\frac{1}{4}$ teaspoon allspice
1   tablespoon orris root
$\frac{1}{4}$ teaspoon anise seed
1   tablespoon each tangerine and lemon rind, grated and
        dried

This is a beautiful mix of subtle fragrances. Leave the top of the jar off for a half-hour before your dinner guests arrive, and the room they enter will have a unique and special aroma.

ᴘᴘᴧ Thyme and Mint Potpourri

½ cup dried rose petals
A few tablespoons dried lily of the valley blossoms
(if you can get them from your garden or the
florist)
The rinds of a tangelo, a tangerine, or an orange, cut
in small strips and dried thoroughly
The dried, slivered rind of a lemon
2 crushed bay leaves
A few crushed, dried thyme leaves
A few crushed, dried mint leaves
1 teaspoon orris root
¼ teaspoon nutmeg
¼ teaspoon cloves
1 pinch allspice
3 tablespoons of sea salt
½ teaspoon oil of bergamot

Mix well all these ingredients except the salt and bergamot. In the
bottom of the jar, put first a layer of salt, then a layer of leaves, then
more salt, and then more leaves. Add the bergamot, a drop at a time.
Keep the jar closed for several days, then open and give the ingredients a good stirring. Do this every few days for a couple of weeks
until potpourri is set.

ᴘᴘᴧ Rosemary Potpourri

1 teaspoon dried mint leaves
1 teaspoon dried tarragon
1 teaspoon dried rosemary

1   tablespoon orris root
3   drops oil of bergamot

Be sure all the herbs are thoroughly dry. Mix all together and put in a covered jar.

If you grow a few roses, it's a simple and pleasant procedure to dry the petals for use in these herb potpourris instead of buying them. The most fragrant and best roses are the old-fashioned cabbage variety or the many-petaled damask rose. But you can use any that are particularly fragrant. Those which are the most scented are found in the sunniest, most protected part of the garden, where they are able to develop their essential oils to the highest degree. After two or three days of dry weather, and before the sun is high in the heavens, gather the flowers you are going to use. Pick those that are just opening, never blossoms that have been out for several days or that have been in the house. Separate the petals and dry them on cake racks or wire netting or screening, raised to let the air circulate beneath. Petals must be in a thin layer, preferably not overlapping. Let each become dry as a cornflake before you use it. If you dry petals in shade they hold their colors better but take longer than those laid out in the sun.

Orris root and oil of benzoin are fixatives that hold the fragrance of dried petals over a period of many months and sometimes years.

Some of the oils that add greatly to potpourris if a few drops are used include oil of geranium, eucalyptus, rosemary, lemon verbena, bergamot, and peppermint. Here's an opportunity to experiment. Try a drop or two of each of several oils in a mix of your own devising.

I consider these recipes and suggestions as a place to begin, not end—an invitation to your imagination and originality. You will probably never make two potpourris exactly alike, nor do you really have to. Small jars for special friends make wonderful gifts at Christmas if there are enough herbs in your window to permit the necessary trimming.

19
The wonder of it

GROWING HERBS INDOORS STIRS ALL THE SENSES—ANYWAY, four of them and, if your imagination is keen, maybe even the fifth as well. First of all, herbs are so charming and appealing to look at. What is more heartening and pleasant to live with than a window full of flourishing herbs? How beautiful they are in the sunshine, with the sun's rays glinting gold over the leaves. On cloudy and stormy days, herb plants bring the green of the outdoors inside to live with you. After you have just watered them, drops glow on the foliage—drops seemingly touched with silver.

Feel or handle the plants and their fragrance fills the room and lingers on your fingers. At all times the fresh, living aroma of growth itself hovers over the window herb garden. How varied and different is the texture of each plant. And what a pleasure it is to touch them—some feathery, some firm and shiny, others soft and downy. Then there is the delicious flavor they impart to all foods. So we have exercised our sight, our sense of smell, of touch, and of taste.

And the fifth sense?

Some morning, after you have just sprinkled your herbs, and the sun is streaming in, imagine you hear them growing—a leaf uncurling, a tendril stretching toward the light! It's not a sound you could possibly reproduce, but surely it's there. Listen!

If you have chameleons in the herb garden, you will certainly hear the gentle rustle of these fascinating small creatures as they move from plant to plant, seeking their dinner of white flies and mealy bugs. Chameleons do for the indoor garden, in a way, what birds do for the outdoor garden. They bring to it movement and life and added interest.

What a pleasure it is to wander outdoors in the garden in midsummer, basket in hand, and gather vegetables for dinner. Now it's almost winter, and the garden is dead and gone. Soon it may be two feet under snow, if you live in the north. No matter. There is something to replace these idyllic moments— moments outdoors, picking beets, and lettuce, and sweet corn —something that, in a delightful sort of way, is subtly suggestive of these harvests of summertime.

Wander over to your indoor herb garden, scissors and small bowl in hand. While the fragrances of all the different plants rise around you, you find yourself admiring the shape of this one, the gray-green tone of that, and the stockiness of yet another one. Now you are snipping small bits and scraps, a leaf here and a stalk there.

Perhaps, after a few moments, you set your bowl and scissors down and draw up a chair beside the indoor garden. For a few moments you have stepped into another world, a world of live greenery and of growth. Ruminating on some of the past histories of the plants, and on what you have learned about them, will put you in a dreamy mood. Perhaps for brief seconds you are transported on a magic carpet back to the days of herb strewing and love charms. But not for long, because today is now, and here is where we belong. Sitting beside this small indoor Eden puts you in a wonderful mood. How soothing and peaceful it is, here in your private tropic. How lovely it is to study each plant, every one quite different from its neighbor, yet each important in itself, an individual and still a part of the whole.

As you consider every herb, perhaps you discover new leaves unfurling and find yourself appreciating the fine details, sensing the wonder in Nature's every design and pattern.

Raising herbs indoors is a complete joy—the beauty, the fragrances, the way the plants feel, the added, exotic flavors in your food. But even more than all that is the pleasure of working with these plants, the care you give them, and their response to you. It is this giving and receiving, this mutual exchange between you and Nature, that draws you close to the heart and core of growth itself. And it is this that becomes so thoroughly satisfying.

Bibliography

Clarkson, Rosetta. *Herbs: Their Culture and Uses.* New York: Macmillan, 1966.

Coats, Alice M. *Flowers and Their Histories.* New York: McGraw-Hill, 1970.

Geuter, Maria. *Herbs in Nutrition.* London: Biodynamic Agricultural Association Anthroposophic Press, 1962.

Grieve, M. *Modern Herbal.* Darien, Conn.: Hafner Publishers, 1931.

Hatfield, Audrey Wynne. *Pleasures of Herbs.* New York: St. Martin's Press, 1965.

Macleod, Dawn. *A Book of Herbs.* London: Duckworth Press, 1968.

Rohde, Eleanour Sinclair. *A Garden of Herbs.* New York: Dover Publications, 1969.

Simmons, Adelma Grenier. *Herb Gardening in Five Seasons.* New York: Van Nostrand Reinhold, 1964.

Taylor, Norman. *Herbs in the Garden.* New York: Van Nostrand Reinhold, 1953.

Index